THE EFFECTIVE INTERPRETING SERIES

ASL Skills Development

Teacher's Guide

Carol J. Patrie, Ph.D.

DawnSignPress

San Diego, California

**The Effective Interpreting Series: ASL Skills Development
Teacher's Guide**

Producer: Joe W. Dannis

Printed in the United States of America

Published by DawnSignPress

Rosetta Stone image © Copyright The British Museum. The Rosetta Stone appears throughout the series as a symbol of translation's importance to mankind. The basalt slab was discovered in July 1799 in the small Egyptian village of Rosette on the western delta of the Nile. The stone's inscription in hieroglyphic, demotic, and Greek languages led to a crucial breakthrough in research regarding Egyptian hieroglyphs. This key to "translating silent images" into a living language symbolizes the importance of accurate transmissions of messages from one language into another.

The Rosetta Stone now resides in the British Museum in London.

Cover Design: Greg Smith

ISBN-10: 1-58121-107-4

ISBN-13: 978-1-58121-107-8

10   9   8   7   6   5   4   3   2   1

For Rebecca Ryan, may Grace bless
her every breath and footstep.

Acknowledgments

As an author it is my privilege and honor to acknowledge all those who have assisted in the development and production of this book. The inspiration for *The Effective Interpreting Series* occurred literally "in a flash." Fortunately for me, and for the field of interpreter education, Joe Dannis continues to believe in me and my vision. We have been working together on these materials since 1995. I am grateful to Joe and his unwavering commitment to my creativity. He has had courage and generosity to support this long-term and ongoing project with all its unexpected twists and turns. He is the steady hand in the background behind *The Effective Interpreting Series.*

I experience gratitude again as I realize that many people at DawnSign Press worked diligently and patiently over time to bring this book to publication. One of the hallmarks of DawnSignPress products is high quality video. The DVD associated with this book is no exception. High quality videos and DVDs are essential in interpreter education. I thank all those involved in filming and video editing. In addition, I thank the accounting department, marketing staff, convention staff, editorial staff, and warehouse staff for their kindnesses and support.

I am grateful to all the speakers who took time from their busy schedules to be videotaped for this project.

I offer especially warm and heartfelt thanks to Rebecca Ryan who has seen all six books in *The Effective Interpreting Series* from first draft to publication. This is a huge feat and she has undertaken the development and editing of each volume with insight and precision. She has remained dedicated to the project with devotion and clarity, and we have learned to dance some intricate steps together along the way, alternating as leader and follower. She stands cheerfully beside me through the good and bad weather of a writer's life. Once again she has borne witness to the birth of a book.

I am especially grateful for the tremendous amount of positive feedback on previous volumes in *The Effective Interpreting Series* from teachers, students, and interpreters. I am thrilled to bring you the sixth volume in the series. I hope you will enjoy it and I look forward to your valuable feedback.

Contents

Preface

When I became a professional interpreter in 1968, interpreter education was rare. Since that time, interpreter education has made great strides. Soon after my first year of professional interpreting in 1968, I began attempting to teach interpreting. From that time to now, I have been building a store of ideas and materials related to teaching interpretation. I am pleased to share with you my 38 years of experience. I am one of the developers of the Master of Arts in Interpretation at Gallaudet University, where I taught interpretation from 1984 to 2000. I am now the Director of Curriculum and Instruction for The Effective Interpreting Professional Education Series at Language Matters, Inc. I am enthusiastic about developing interpreter education materials and providing up-to-date training for interpreters and interpreter educators and welcome your feedback on this and other volumes in the series.

See www.language-matters.com for additional information on credit courses offered by Language Matters that address the topics in *The Effective Interpreting Series.* LMI also offers graduate level courses on teaching interpreting.

The exercises presented in this book result from my desire to develop materials practicing and future interpreters can use in or out of the classroom while studying simultaneous interpretation. This book can be used independently of any other book in *The Effective Interpreting Series,* or it can be used as one of the sequence of five books that provide a systematic approach to developing skills in simultaneous interpreting from ASL.

In my experience I have found that one of the greatest challenges in interpreter education for signed or spoken language is finding or creating appropriate materials for use in the classroom. An even more severe problem is overcoming the lack of study materials that practicing and future interpreters can use on their own, either for refresher practice or for continuing professional development. There is a growing demand for mentorship in both signed and spoken language interpretation and materials to optimize these contacts.

Simultaneous interpreting is a very complex skill that requires intensive and appropriate practice. It is my hope that by providing materials for developing interpreting skills from ASL, practicing and future interpreters will find the process of developing interpretation skills to be rewarding and effective.

Successful interpreters rely on many skills in their everyday work. The development of these skills is not intuitive or automatic. Simultaneous interpreting must be developed through a careful sequence of learning activities. Isolating specific skills and learning them one at a time is the best approach to learning complex new skills. Learning new skills one at a time allows mastery of individual skills and a feeling of success. Gaining control over components of the interpretation process can assist in developing simultaneous interpreting skills because appropriate practice helps to routinize these complex skills. The skills that make up the simultaneous interpreting processes are generally not used in isolation and must be synthesized correctly in order to render an interpretation.

Component skills for simultaneous interpreting are interactive and interdependent. The learning process should begin with strengthening skills in your first language (L1) and move in a carefully structured sequence from intralingual skill development to *inter*lingual development. The first five volumes in *The Effective Interpreting Series* provide English source materials and exercises that focus on cognitive processing, English skills development, translation, and consecutive and simultaneous interpreting. This volume, the first in the ASL series, provides practice materials designed to enhance ASL skills needed for ASL-English interpretation.

Description of the Materials

This set of materials includes a teacher's guide and a student study set. The teacher's guide includes all of the information in the student study set plus instructions for the teacher. The books refer to the exercises on the DVD. What makes this volume unique is that you will answer the study questions in ASL. The ASL intralingual skills in this study set focus on finding the main idea, summarizing, lexical substitution, paraphrasing, and form and meaning. Throughout the entire volume there is a strong emphasis on developing reliable comprehension skills because comprehension forms the basis for faithful interpretations.

The DVD

The DVD contains video segments that are to be used with the book. The directions for each exercise tell you when to watch the DVD and how to provide your answers. The DVD has been designed to offer access to the video segments that correspond to the specific exercises and questions.

The DVD opens with a title page.

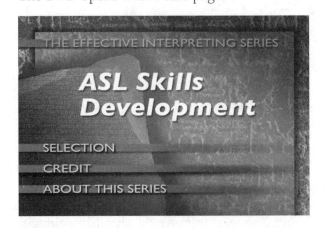

The Selection menu lists all of the Units.

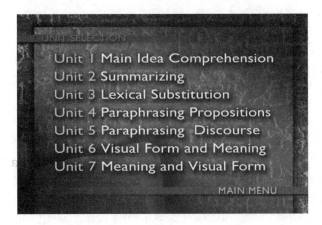

The Exercise menus guide you to the specific segment you need to complete the exercise. Many of the exercises have a segment called Get to Know the Signer. Each exercise has clips where signers tell a story, or give sentence level information in ASL.

Here is an example of the Exercise menu.

Not all exercises have all types of segments, but here is an explanation of the possible parts of each exercise.

Get to Know the Signer

Some exercises have a short segment where the signer introduces himself or herself. There are comprehension questions related to these segments. The story titles are used as the title of the exercise.

The Story

In each exercise the signer tells a story or gives information in ASL.

Study Questions

This part is where you answer questions regarding the signer's story. This element on the DVD shows up for Units 1, 2, and 3. For these units specific parts of the video segments relate to study questions. If the book shows a video capture, there will be a segment on the DVD to help you answer that question.

The short clips that relate to the study questions are broken down at sentence or idea level. There are times when one clip includes information for several study questions. In these instances, the numbers for the questions are grouped together. After each study question clip is done playing, the DVD returns you to the exercise menu and highlights the clip you have just seen. This functions as "play again." If you wish to view the clip several times, simply play the clip again at the menu. If you are done answering the questions related to a clip, use your DVD remote or the controls for your DVD software to select the next study question or group of questions to continue.

In the book, the questions with a related clip include a video capture and time code to help you focus on the exact part of the video needed to answer the question.

01:01:36;09

Some Units only have a Get to Know the Signer segment and the story. Here is an example from Unit seven.

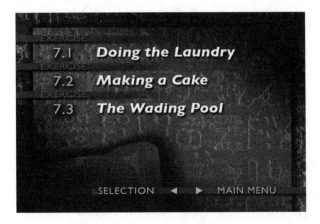

At the bottom of the screen in every unit page in the DVD is a navigation bar that has a link to the unit selection, and the main menu, along with arrows that take you to the previous page, and the next page.

Introduction to the Teacher's Guide

Why This Approach?

One of the reasons that the study of the interpretation process has been so challenging is that the nature of the interpretation process itself has resisted definition and description. Without descriptors of the interpretation process, it has been difficult for teachers of interpretation to effect predictable change in student performance as a result of contact with interpreter education curricula. Fortunately, in recent years there has been much research into the nature of interpretation. There are a number of models of the interpretation process. No two are exactly alike, but all models suggest that the interpretation process is a multi-stage process (Moser-Mercer, 1997). As Gile (2005) points out, there are at least two broad categories of models. Some models are used to describe the interpretation process to help researchers better understand the process and other models are best suited to teaching about the interpretation process.

Gonzalez et al. (1991, p. 335) propose the Simultaneous Human Information Processing Model. This model is quite different from other models because it is three-dimensional and portrayed in a circular rather than a linear fashion and incorporates principles of more linear models into a more powerful model. (Please see Gonzales et al., 1991, for a fuller description.) Another point that Moser-Mercer makes is that even though most researchers will agree that interpretation is a multi-stage process, they do not agree on the names of the stages or the contents of the stages. In her conclusion, Moser-Mercer states that "A powerful model of the interpreting process must be broad enough to include aspects that reflect the complex, time constrained multitasking environment of simultaneous interpreting that involves a high degree of cognitive processing" (Moser-Mercer, 1997, p. 194). For detailed information on the models mentioned, please refer to the chapter by Moser-Mercer in the reference by Danks et al. (1997).

The student study set was developed along the lines of Gile's (1995) model because it provides a clear and simple framework for the importance of understanding how best to organize your effort while interpreting. Gile suggests that in the process of learning interpretation, it makes sense to routinize processes where possible because there is limited capacity for specific aspects of the interpretation process, and these capacities must be greater than what the interpretation process requires. By mastering intralingual skills before moving to the more complex skills required in simultaneous interpreting, students will ensure an adequate capacity for that part of the interpretation process.

Basic Assumptions about Interpreter Education

There are several assumptions about interpreter education that form the basis of this text. These assumptions are derived from the work of many interpreter educators who have published their work via The Conference of Interpreter Trainers, American Translators Association, or the John Benjamin's Translation Library. I am strongly in favor of these assumptions and I used them as the basis for my work in teaching interpretation over the past 38 years. The first assumption is that tasks that are relatively less cognitively demanding should appear in the curriculum and be mastered prior to tasks that are more demanding. For example, cognitive tasks such as immediate and delayed repetition and pattern inference are thought to be easier or more manageable for new interpreting students than more demanding tasks such as consecutive or simultaneous interpreting. (A discussion of these terms is provided in the student study set.) The second assumption is that mastery of tasks at a certain level indicates readiness to move on to a more difficult level. The third assumption is that training should proceed from intralingual exercises that may be taught concurrently with cognitive exercises to translation. Consecutive interpreting should follow translation, which in turn should be followed by simultaneous interpreting. Both monologic and dialogic skill development should be addressed.

A fourth assumption is that interpreters must have high levels of intralingual proficiency. Drills and skills in ASL are often overlooked and neglected in interpreter education programs. This may be due to the enormous amount of material that must be covered in the interpreter education curriculum, leaving little time for ensuring the development of strong ASL skills. However, it is absolutely essential that interpreter educators maintain a strong stand on developing ASL skills in potential interpreters *before* attempting to develop the other skills needed to become an interpreter. When interpreter educators insist on well-developed, well-controlled ASL skills, students will also realize the importance of high levels of ASL proficiency.

In addition to above-average ASL proficiency skills, interpreters must have high levels of cognitive manipulation skills. Intralingual skills and cognitive manipulation skills underlie the more complex skill of simultaneous interpreting. The development of these skills can reduce the amount of effortful processing that is needed to perform these component skills. Lessons and educational experiences that are logically sequenced can lead to more effective learning and teaching experiences. A logical sequence could begin with designing a curriculum, the courses in it, and the lessons within the courses and then teaching the individual lessons. Next the teacher must evaluate the success of the lessons by looking at both student and teacher outcomes. The next logical step is to provide feedback to students that will allow them to improve their outcomes. Then the teacher can plan the subsequent lesson. This teacher's guide is designed to help you follow a logical sequence in teaching and evaluating ASL skills as they relate to developing the interpreting process.

These assumptions regarding the appropriate sequencing of experiences in interpreter education and the importance of strong skills in one's first language (L1) and second language (L2) underlie all of the information and exercises that follow. Effective interpreter training can lead to enhanced job satisfaction. Greater job satisfaction for individuals can lead to improved levels of professionalism. Improved levels of professionalism among interpreters can ultimately lead to greater consumer satisfaction.

How to Use the Teacher's Guide

This teacher's guide consists of the student study set plus directions and ideas for the teacher. Information intended for the teacher is presented in *italics* in each unit. The *italicized* information includes teaching ideas as well as possible answers to the exercises. Teachers are encouraged to expand on the instructional ideas presented here. Write your own teaching ideas in the margins and spaces provided. Careful planning of meaningful exercises can make instructional time more valuable for teachers and students. Please read "How to Use the Student Study Set" to be sure you and your students have the same understanding about using the book. Ideally, you will read the entire student text and review the video before using either with your students. This preview will allow you to be fully aware of the content of the book and video.

Each unit has an introduction section and a section that explains the relevance of that concept to the interpretation process. In each unit there are discussion questions for you to use to orient students to the concepts before beginning the exercises. The exercises have directions for you in italics and directions for the students. The directions to the teacher appear only in the first exercise in each unit, but should be followed for each exercise in that unit. In some cases, English translations of possible responses are provided to guide the teacher. The length of time of each video selection is included in the directions. You may want to do a dry run with the DVD and exercises to determine how many exercises can be done during class time and how many can be assigned for homework. Some exercises can be done in group format and others require individual recordings by students and are best done individually. The first exercise is designed to be an in-class warm-up to ensure that students understand how to do the work. The second exercise could be used for homework, while the third and more challenging exercise could be used for grading purposes or additional homework. There are study questions for each exercise. A progress tracking sheet is included at the end of each unit. The tracking sheet allows students to have a consistent place to record the dates of their work and questions related to the work. The tracking sheet also allows you to monitor student progress easily. You can ask students to make a copy of the tracking sheet when it is completed and submit it to you for review.

It is customary in most academic settings to present the grading policies in the course syllabus, which should be distributed to student interpreters on the first day of class. This can help students and teachers to be clear as to what is expected and when assignments are due. Keep in mind that you will want to clarify your polices regarding work that is submitted after the due date. In interpreter training curricula it is very important that students keep up with the scheduled work.

Analyzing Student Work

In general, most colleges and interpreter training programs must award grades to students who are enrolled in courses. The area of grading student performance is usually one of the most difficult aspects of teaching interpretation. Naturally, we would all prefer to have a non-evaluative approach when working with students. Nevertheless, sometimes student interpreters do not perform at levels that predict success later in the curriculum and possibly in the profession. Teachers of interpretation have an obligation to the profession as a whole to provide student interpreters with accurate and meaningful feedback experiences that are supportive, encouraging, and informative. At the same time, teachers want student interpreters to develop accuracy and autonomy in monitoring their own work. This text provides approaches for tracking student progress and encouraging the development of independent and accurate self-monitoring skills by asking students to take responsibility for their work immediately. Accountability for one's work is accomplished via timely completion of the exercises, answering the study questions, and filling in the tracking sheets.

It is important to decide in advance of teaching the course which exercises will be graded, how they will be graded, and how individual exercise grades affect the overall grade. The time taken to generate a reasoned approach to tracking student progress will ultimately save time for both student interpreters and teachers. Similar grading polices used in each program's curriculum will also result in time savings and lead to a more satisfying semester or quarter for all involved. Naturally, grading policies must be consistent and uniform for all students enrolled in a course.

Ideally, exercises are presented in the context of a course and the course is presented in the context of a curriculum. Content of individual courses should be developed with the overall goals of the curriculum in mind. The outcomes of each course should lead to the beginning point of the course that follows. All courses in the curriculum should lead to the mastery of curricular goals.

Feedback to Students

A teacher or mentor should provide timely feedback and guidance to students. Students and novices in any field can benefit from guidance from a more experienced practitioner. That guidance is generally difficult to provide in a meaningful way in interpreter education classes if the class size is over 10. The Conference of Interpreter Trainers has published a position paper that states that the ideal class size for interpreter education is 6 to 10 students (1998). Unfortunately, in many programs, the class size is indeed more than 10. With that current reality in mind, this text has been created in such a way as to have the students take responsibility for their work at certain levels of review and analysis. However, even if the process is streamlined, the importance of the role of direct input from teacher to student with meaningful guidance for improvement cannot be minimized. A few suggestions are provided here to assist teachers with the important process of providing meaningful guidance to students.

Teachers can remember to comment directly on the work and not the student. Commenting on the work will, in turn, encourage students to do the same. This objectivity will be useful to students, as they eventually become peer supports for each other as classmates and later as professional colleagues. As a result of having clearly planned exercises at hand, teachers can focus more closely on exactly what student performances should look like. This will lead to more immediate and meaningful feedback.

It is essential for teachers to provide accurate and meaningful feedback as early in the interpreter education program as possible. All too often, we have seen students who are minimally qualified as interpreters somehow pass each course in the program and graduate with a degree or certificate. Every interpreter educator has had the experience of seeing a student graduate who clearly had minimal aptitude and ability for interpretation, but the program and the courses in it had no way of weeding out students who were not progressing satisfactorily. This teacher's guide, student book, and video provide assistance in quantifying student performances in a meaningful way.

Teachers can help students develop insight into the processes used in the exercises. Even if a student says "I don't know how or why that is my answer," the teacher can help students gain insight into how they arrived at that decision. Since it is crucial to develop insight into the process of interpretation, the teacher can explain his or her own processes and make these processes explicit in order to help students see the many components and decisions that are a part of the interpretation process. Further information regarding teaching interpretation is available in some of the citations listed at the end of this work.

Equipment and Language Laboratory Ideas

The process of learning to interpret requires the use of specific audiovisual equipment. First, I describe the ideal situation and then the minimum requirements. Programs are encouraged to obtain the best possible equipment in sufficient quantities so that the instructional contact time during the interpreter education program is maximized.

The ideal situation is a language lab with a carrel for each student or possibly one carrel for two students. In each carrel should be a video camera that records what the student is saying or signing onto a local recording device in that student carrel. There should be a second playback device (DVD or VHS) and a monitor with good resolution. The recording device should allow the student to record source language and target language simultaneously onto a single videotape or DVD. Each carrel should have a headphone that allows the student to hear either the source or the target language. The headset may have a microphone built in or there may be a separate microphone to record the student's voice. An intercom system allows the student and teacher to interact via voice or sign without interfering with other students. A high-quality audiocassette recorder should be an integral part of each carrel.

The ideal teacher's console should allow the teacher to group students or allow each student to work independently. The teacher's console should allow the teacher to broadcast source material to some or all students. An intercom system allows the teacher to call on an individual student without disturbing other students. The console should also allow the teacher to listen and watch each student work without interrupting him or her. It should also be possible for the teacher to record samples of student work at the teacher console. The teacher should be able to speak to the entire class at once through the system.

At a minimum the program should provide a playback device (DVD or VCR) and monitor for each student as well as one camera for every one or two students. This arrangement does not allow source and target to be recorded simultaneously but it does allow students to record their own work during class time. It also does not allow the teacher to interact privately with each student.

In either the ideal lab or the minimal lab, adequate space is required for the equipment so students can work without interfering with each other. In situations where the program cannot provide adequate space and equipment for interpreter education, students in those programs will be required to own equipment or have access to equipment. Specifically, each student will need access to a VCR or DVD player, monitor, camera, and audio recorder. These equipment requirements should be made clear to prospective students before they enter the program. Many programs are moving toward digital media and media players. In order to reduce confusion, it is important that program managers and faculty let students know in advance of entering the program if they will need to own or have access to specific equipment in order to be able to do the work required in each course.

The approach to interpreter education used here is a highly interactive one that is based on research and theory, but is reliant on frequent and meaningful interaction between students and their teachers. The approaches to analysis, feedback, and the sample rating system are suggested as guidelines. Feel free to incorporate these or modify them to suit your teaching style.

The student study set starts here. Directions to the teacher are interwoven in italics in the student study set.

Introduction to ASL Skills Development

The Importance of ASL Language Skills

This study set focuses on development of skills within ASL. Many authors have written about the importance of language competence in interpreter and translator education. When skills are developed *within* a language, these skills are called *intralingual*. When the skills are mastered and effectively used, then language competence is present. In developing mastery of intralingual skills, it is best to begin in one's first language (L1). Roda Roberts (1992) says, "Language competency, which covers the ability to manipulate with ease and accuracy the *two* languages involved in the interpreting process, is a prerequisite for successful interpreting of a message, for the message is mediated through language" (p.1 emphasis added). She further subdivides the idea of language competency by saying that language competency includes the "ability to understand the source language in all its nuances and the ability to express oneself correctly, fluently, clearly and with poise in the target language" (p. 2).

It is clear that intralingual skills must be well developed in both languages used in the interpretation process. When intralingual skills are well developed, the amount of effort needed for processing information is less. Since simultaneous interpreting is a very difficult task, it is best to reduce the amount of effort needed by mastering the component skills before combining them into the more cognitively complex skills needed for simultaneous interpretation.

Moser-Mercer (1984) suggests that competence in monolingual exercises, or exercises within one language, can be a predictor for determining success in interpreter training (p.43). Arjona (1984) says, "The complexity of the communication process in which a translation or interpretation practitioner must function requires nothing less than superior mastery of the language systems involved. Anything less jeopardizes the standards of performance which of necessity must be professionally assured" (p. 3). Arjona suggests that the goal of interpreter training programs is to allow graduates to function with a "minimum competency, proficiency and mastery level needed to perform successfully in real life situations" (p.3). She explains that the term "minimum competency" does not mean rock bottom. She uses minimum competency to mean being able to meet the minimum requirement for mastering the task.

She goes on to say that candidates for graduation from an interpreter education program must be able to "routinely translate or interpret the message accurately and appropriately, thus bridging the communication gap in a meaningful manner" (p.6). This means that each individual graduating from a program must be able to perform well against standards for entry to the profession.

In 1994, I conducted a national survey of Project Directors of Federally funded interpreter training grants (Patrie, 1994). I asked these leaders in the field whether there was a "readiness-to-work -gap." Another way to look at this question is to ask whether program exit standards match up with the requirements of entry to the profession. "In response to the survey, the project directors stated unequivocally that this gap exists. They report that as educators, they observe that at the end of interpreter education programs, few graduates are employment-ready. As employers of interpreters, they report that recent program graduates often do not have the necessary skills to enter the job market" (p.53).

In order to have reliable interpretation skills upon graduation in interpretation it is essential to provide a strong sequence of activities that lead to language enhancement and interpreting skills. It is generally the case that both English and ASL skills will need improvement during interpreter education in order to ensure reliable interpretation skills upon program completion. When a new interpreter is well prepared to enter the job market, it is likely that this interpreter will demonstrate high levels of professionalism. Higher levels of professionalism can lead to greater consumer satisfaction and greater recognition of the profession of interpretation overall.

Goal of This Study Set

The purpose of the study set is to improve and enhance your ASL skills before attempting to interpret from or to ASL. It is important to develop ASL skills with conscious effort, regardless of whether ASL is your first or second language. This study set provides you with specific skills that will build confidence in your ASL skills. As you use this study set, you will improve not only your skills, but also your awareness of the importance of ASL skills.

An increased awareness of ASL usage leads to a more reliable interpretation. A reliable interpretation naturally communicates as much as possible of the original meaning. So, it is important to be sure that the meaning of the original message has been correctly analyzed and understood, insofar as conditions permit. The seven units in this study set are specially designed to provide practice in the intralingual skills in ASL that will help insure that the message is correctly understood and analyzed. Strong intralingual skills in ASL are a stepping stone to professional level interpretation skills.

The simultaneous interpretation process is not actually a linear sequence of skills that are performed one at a time. The various parts of the simultaneous interpretation process, listening, analyzing, transferring the message into another language, and finding expression for that idea, all interact with each other as the signer continues speaking and the interpreter continues interpreting. It can be overwhelming and not very successful to try to master all parts of the process at once. Instead, it is more effective to learn how to master the component skills in the interpretation process and then synthesize the component skills into the process of simultaneous interpretation.

Just as the overall process of interpretation is not really linear, the component skills are not linear either. During the actual process of interpretation, specific ASL skills are dynamic and interact with each other and with other processes. ASL skills do not appear as discrete units in the interpretation process. Seven important ASL skills are presented in this study set. These ASL skills are separated into seven units in this study set for two reasons. Learning to manage the components of the process and then synthesizing them is an effective approach to learning a complex skill. The second reason for separating the skills and studying them one at a time is to promote the easy identification of any problem area. Separating the component skills allows you to experience mastery of the components of the larger process.

Why Intralingual ASL Skills Are Important

In addition to strong intralingual skills, interpreters must have high levels of cognitive manipulation skills. Intralingual skills and cognitive manipulation skills are two of the skills that underlie the more complex skill of simultaneous interpreting. The development of these skills can reduce the amount of effortful processing that is needed to perform these component skills. According to Kohn and Kalina (1996) in Massaro and Shlesinger (1997), " Automation of strategic processes also plays an important role, for only if routine decision processes are performed more or less automatically will the interpreter have enough capacity and attention to solve the more intricate and complex linguistic problems."

Gonzalez et al. (1991) emphasize the importance of routinization, or making conscious acts become more automatic. A skill that once demanded much effort and attention can become unconscious over time with practice. "Conscious attention to the interpreting task thereafter may actually interfere with performance" (p.333). As the interpretation process becomes more routinized, less effort is needed. After interpreters acquire the skill, it is difficult for them to describe what is actually happening. Even when interpreters have managed to make many of the processes in interpretation more automatic, interpretation is still a highly demanding and cognitively complex task. When the component skills are routinized, overall interpretation performance improves.

The systematic development of the intralingual skills that underlie the interpretation process is very important. If these skills are not developed and available, then there is a much higher chance that the skills that must follow such as translation, consecutive interpretation, and simultaneous interpretation will not be strongly grounded. The resulting deficit could lead to interpretations that are skewed or that contain errors. When more advanced skills do not have a firm base, more effortful processing is required during the interpretation process. When more effortful processing is needed, the likelihood of fatigue is increased. Increased fatigue leads to a corresponding increase in errors in interpretation.

Quick access to intralingual skills underlies many of the more complicated aspects of the interpretation process. Interpreters must be able to quickly make sense out of what they see and hear, and decide what the message means and how to transfer that message into another language with split-second accuracy. Shreve and Koby (1997) point out that during the past 25 years, there has been much interest in trying to describe the processes associated with interpreting. They point out that these mental operations are largely "hidden," yet form a complex and essential part of the interpretation process. One way to look at these hidden aspects of the interpretation process is to study models of interpretation. Models of interpretation are theoretical. These models attempt to describe the process of interpretation and how the process might affect the product of the interpretation.

Models of the Interpretation Process

There are a number of models of the interpretation process. No two are exactly alike, but all models suggest that the interpretation process is a multi-stage process. Gile (2005 MIIS Conference) notes that some models are really designed by and for researchers and may not be all that helpful to students learning the process, while other models are designed to help students understand and better manage the process.

> "Over the past decades, the scholarly field of Translation Studies has been gaining an increasingly higher profile in translator and interpreter training programs, and translation theories and models are often invoked, taught and/or discussed even in those institutions which in the past tended to ignore them. However, perhaps due to the fact that integration of theoretical thinking in T&I training has not reached sufficient maturity yet, there is some confusion about the features of and requirements from theoretical elements depending on their role. Broadly speaking, theories for training achieve their purposes best if they help students make sense of phenomena they experience and guide their strategies and learning process, whereas theories for research achieve their purpose best if they help researchers explain and predict phenomena and are testable and open-ended so as to allow gradual fine-tuning and/or replacement by more accurate theories. Thus, simple non-testable or even deliberately inaccurate theoretical metaphors may be powerful as didactic tools but of little use in research, whereas testable complex theoretical systems may be appropriate for research purposes but of doubtful adequacy for training purposes." (Gile, 2005, conference program book)

Moser-Mercer (1997) summarizes some of the better known models of interpretation. She mentions the following models among others: Gerver, 1976; Moser-Mercer, 1978; Kitano, 1993; and a summary of Daro and Fabbro's 1994 model of memory during interpretation. Moser-Mercer points out that many models use an information processing approach to explain the interpretation process. Information systems models are based on computer-style operations. This kind of analysis will be necessarily somewhat flawed since human minds do not operate exactly like computers. Another point that Moser-Mercer makes is that even though most researchers will agree that interpretation is a multi-stage process, they do not agree on the names of the stages or the contents of the stages. Moser-Mercer states that " A powerful model of the interpreting process must be broad enough to include aspects that reflect the complex, time constrained multitasking environment of simultaneous interpreting that involves a high degree of cognitive processing" (Moser, 1997, p. 194). For detailed information on the models mentioned, please refer to the chapter by Moser-Mercer in Danks (1997).

Regardless of which model of interpretation you choose to study, you will soon see that all models require that the incoming message be analyzed and understood before any part of the transfer process can begin. In order to accomplish an accurate analysis of the incoming ASL message, it is essential to have strong ASL intralingual skills.

In this study set, I emphasize Gile's (1995) Effort Model because it provides a clear and simple framework for the importance of cognitive processing tasks. Gile's Effort Model provides a powerful rationale for developing intralingual skills before learning the interpretation process and is to be viewed in a different light than models that describe stages of the interpreting process in detail.

According to Gile (1995), many of the mental operations required in the interpretation process are non-automatic and require conscious effort. He suggests that there are three main effort areas in the interpretation process: the Listen and Analysis Effort, which deals with comprehension, the Production Effort, which includes speech planning and verbal output, and the Memory Effort, which deals with the stresses placed on the short-term memory system. These three efforts are integrated by the Coordination Effort. Gile also suggests that each interpreter has certain capacities within each of these areas of effort. Ideally, the interpreter has more capacity than is currently required by the interpretation task. This study set provides clear approaches to developing the intralingual skills that support using effort in ways that lead to successful interpretations.

When to Develop ASL Skills

If you are a novice or new interpreter, ASL skills should be developed before moving on to more advanced skills in the interpretation process. If you are beyond the beginning stages of an interpreter education program or are already a practicing interpreter, you can still benefit from practice in ASL skills, either as a refresher or for professional skill maintenance.

The exercises in this book can be used as review and refresher material. Sometimes students in interpreter education programs may experience the "plateau effect" in training. The plateau effect occurs when skills appear to no longer develop as rapidly as they did earlier in the training process.

This is a common occurrence. When progress seems to stagnate, it is often useful to go back to an earlier stage of skill development and practice at that level. Taking time to go back and review skills is a positive step because it increases confidence, builds mastery, and often provides the springboard to further progress.

This study set can also benefit practicing interpreters because it may be used for continuing education credit in an independent study format. Practicing interpreters may not have had the benefit of studying the individual skills that make up the interpretation process. Practicing interpreters often search for specific ways to improve their interpretation skills. Practicing the components of the interpretation process, such as intralingual skills, can be meaningful and productive practice for the experienced interpreter who wishes to work independently on skill improvement. Strong intralingual skills form a good basis for more complex skills in the interpretation process.

The Value of Deliberate Practice

In order to find out what activities should be practiced, Ericsson et al. (1993) identified the training activities most closely associated with optimal improvement of performance and classified them as effective, deliberate practice.

Characteristics of Effective Practice

If practice is the avenue to developing expertise for beginners or more experienced interpreters, it is important to know what kinds of practice will be helpful and how long practice should last. Ericsson's (2001) work focuses on the importance of *effective* practice and says, "Improvement of performance was uniformly observed when individuals, who were motivated to improve their performance, were given well-defined tasks, were provided with feedback, and had ample opportunities for repetition. Individuals were able to keep improving during a series of training sessions as long as the sessions were limited to around an hour—the time college students were able to maintain sufficient concentration to make active efforts to improve" (p. 193). If this idea is applied to interpreter education or working interpreters who wish to improve their skills, it means that exercises must be logically related to relevant interpreting tasks and must be done with deliberate intention.

Ericsson (2001) also emphasizes the importance of *deliberate* practice and notes, "Deliberate efforts include problem solving and finding better methods to perform the tasks" (p. 193). Deliberate practice on appropriate materials is important for improving performance. According to Ericsson (2001, p.194), the main characteristics of deliberate practice are solitary practice with full concentration and the intention to improve certain aspects of performance. For musicians who practiced in this way there were consistent correlations between level of attained performance and amount and quality of solitary activities. To emphasize the importance of the amount of time spent in solitary practice, Ericsson et al. (1993) compared three groups of musicians. The most accomplished musicians had practiced for about 10,000 hours by age 20. Two other groups of musicians who had practiced 5,000 and 2,500 hours, respectively, were ranked second and third in skill compared to the group who had practiced 10,000 hours. "Deliberate practice is important for attaining high levels of skill and also for maintaining expertise. The concept of deliberate practice also accounts for individual differences in the maintenance of expert performance (Krampe and Ericsson, 1996)" (Ericsson, 2001, p. 194). Those who continue in deliberate solitary practice are likely to maintain their expertise.

Self-Confidence

Not only do experts exhibit reliably reproducible performances, but also they tend to have identifiable personality characteristics. Keiser (1978) says that experts have good communication skills and can convince others of their expertise and that these characteristics are a good basis for interpreting expertise. Hoffman (1997) summarizes research on expertise and notes that experts show self-confidence (Bradley, 1981) and are willing to stand behind their decisions (Klemp and McClelland, 1986). Hoffman suggests that interpreting students who do not have self-confidence generally do not progress as well as those who do. Through deliberate, effective practice you can improve your interpreting skills in a systematic way. Knowing that you are taking these steps helps to improve your overall self-confidence and can lead to greater expertise.

Specific ASL Skills

The ASL skills in this book are presented in a sequence that builds in complexity. This sequence of skills optimally is practiced in your first language (L1) (See The Effective Interpreting Series: English Skills Development for L1 practice in English) and then in the second language (L2). Intralingual skills that support the development and maintenance of interpreting skills include finding the main point, summarizing, lexical substitution, paraphrasing, and form and meaning. A description of these skills is presented below. Each of these skills is relevant to any level of experience in interpretation, beginning, intermediate, or advanced.

Terminology

It is important to have a clear understanding of the terminology used in this book. The main terms for each unit are described here.

Discourse Paraphrasing

Discourse paraphrasing means restating a longer text in a different form without changing the meaning. Unit 5 has information and exercises on paraphrasing information at the discourse level and provides opportunities to restate larger amounts of information than occurs at the sentence level. In either sentence or discourse level, the underlying meaning must not be skewed when it is restated.

Distinguishing Main from Supporting Ideas

The main idea in a speech or passage is the central point or single most important idea in the speech or passage. Unit 1 provides exercises and information on sorting main ideas from supporting ideas. These exercises allow you to begin to establish the relative importance of various parts of utterances. In the event that some information must be deleted from the interpretation due to the heavy flow of information, it is important to be able to distinguish which aspects are less important. For example, repetitions and paraphrases of information stated earlier by the signer might be considered of lesser importance than information that only occurs once and is central to the message. Central aspects of the message must not be deleted in the interpretation.

Form and Meaning

Units 6 and 7 deal with the important distinctions between form and meaning. The issue of form and meaning is a complex one. The distinctions between form and meaning are often overlooked, yet these distinctions create the basis for a reliable interpretation.

Form refers to the observable aspects of the language, in this case ASL signs and their arrangement into sentences. The meaning can also be referred to as the message. Seleskovitch and Lederer (1989) say, "the sense," or ideas to be expressed in a specific form or language. The ASL sign is a symbol for the concept or thing to which it refers.

Saussure (1966) proposed the idea of a "linguistic sign" as a way to describe the link between form and concept. "The linguistic sign unites, not a thing and a name, but a concept and a sound-image" (p.66) (from Gonzalez et al., 1991, p. 299). Because form and meaning are so closely linked, the distinctions between the two are not obvious to many people. This is one reason that exercises that focus on the distinction between form and meaning are included in this study set.

Lexical Substitution

Lexical substitution means replacing a word in a specific context with another word that minimizes change to the meaning of the original utterance. Lexical substitution exercises in Unit 3 are designed to improve your vocabulary so that you can quickly replace the original sign with another while preserving the meaning as closely as possible.

Process and Product

In interpreter education there is always much discussion over whether students should focus on the process of the interpretation or the product of the interpretation. Both are equally important and should be part of even the earliest stages of training. It is vital that you understand the difference between these two terms and the role they play in your education and training as an interpreter. The process of interpretation is largely invisible. The process is what goes on in your head as you listen, analyze, and transfer the meaning from one language to another. The product, the message rendered in the target language, is the end result of the process.

The processes associated with the interpretation event cannot be recorded or observed by another person. Only via introspection can the interpreter gain insight into their own process and make changes to it. Gile (1995) suggests that adopting a process-oriented approach can optimize training time. In Gile's opinion it is best not to focus only on the end products of the process, but rather to include information on "principles, methods and procedures" (p.10). Gile goes on to support his idea this way. "By concentrating on the reasons for errors or good choices in Translation rather than on the words or structures produced by the students, teachers devote most of their effective teaching time to translation strategies and lose little time over their by-products" (p.11). Gile goes on to say that later on in interpreter training programs, additional emphasis must be placed on product, but only after the underlying processes are established. Even though the exercises in this book are not interpretation exercises, when you record your answers you will use those answers as the product to analyze.

The product is the observable part of your work. In an interpretation the product is what the "listener" receives from the "sender" via your interpretation. The product can be recorded for future analysis, while the process cannot. Seal has summarized the results of a recent study of interpreters who wished to improve their skills. In that report, she emphasizes the importance of analyzing one's own work. "Self-analysis, the zenith of any professional development activity, is highly facilitated when we step back and take a look at ourselves. Routine videotaping and observing videotaped performances for strengths and weaknesses and for changes over time is quite possibly the most valuable, yet least frequently accomplished activity we can engage in" (Seal, 1999 p. 14).

Propositional Paraphrasing

Paraphrasing means restating the message in a different way (form), which attempts to preserve the meaning as closely as possible. Unit 4 provides exercises in propositional paraphrasing. These exercises provide practice in unpacking or discovering the possible meanings contained in specific utterances.

Summarization

A summary is a brief rendition of the most important points in a passage. A summary can be as short as one sentence, which is sometimes called the gist of the passage, or it could be as long as a paragraph in the case of a longer text. Unit 2 provides exercises in creating concise and accurate summaries to allow you to focus on the most important aspect of the message. In some cases when the information load forces the interpreter to be farther behind the message than is ideal, summarizing can sometimes be used to catch up. Occasionally a consumer may request a summary interpretation. A summary interpretation provides only the main points and is usually provided after the source language has stopped. Summarization skills are important as a developmental tool as well as a professional tool.

Visual Form

The term "visual form" can refer to a printed picture or visualization. It is a representation of an idea but does not use words to convey the idea. Pictures are used in some of the exercises to help you understand that the picture of an idea is not the same thing as the expression of that idea in ASL. Although the idea "behind" the picture and corresponding visualization could be the same, the form is different when an idea is expressed in a picture and when it is expressed in ASL. It is important to realize that form is arbitrary, whether it is a printed word, sign, visualization, or picture. "The fact that external form is arbitrary can be seen in the phenomenon of synonyms. Two words can represent the same underlying concept, like 'car' and 'auto' and single words like 'bear' and 'nut' can represent multiple concepts" (Gonzalez et al., 1991, p. 299).

How to Use the Study Set

Information, and exercises, are provided in the seven skill units in this book. The ASL intralingual skills in this study set are main idea, summarizing, lexical substitution, paraphrasing propositions, paraphrasing discourse, relationships between visual form and ASL, and relationships between ASL and visual form. These are some of the important intralingual skills interpreters need. In each unit, a brief introduction provides background information and an explanation of the relevance of that information to the overall interpretation process. The introductory material is followed by a series of exercises specifically designed to help you apply the concepts presented in the unit. In each unit there are two main parts of each exercise. The first is to respond to the exercise material and record your answers. This allows you to create a product. For either independent or group work, this study set provides complete directions for each exercise. The directions guide you to the correct location on the accompanying DVD. The second part of each exercise is to answer the study questions. Answering the study questions allows you to examine your *product* and, in some cases, compare it to that of the signers on the tape. The study questions help provide focus and insight into your responses to the exercises.

All of the exercises (recording your responses and answering the study questions) in each unit may be completed as out-of-classroom work or as independent work during class time, if appropriate equipment is available.

The first exercise in each unit is best used as a warm-up or orientation to the exercises in the unit and can usually be done in class or with a group. The study set exercises provide the opportunity to take responsibility for creating work (product) and to analyze and develop strategies for improvement. In this study set, it is not necessary to translate or interpret any of the ASL messages. All of the exercises in this study set are designed to improve and strengthen skills in understanding meaning in ASL and developing skills in working with ASL.

What You Need before Beginning the Exercises

You will need specific equipment in order to get the maximum benefit from these exercises: a DVD player with a remote control that will allow pausing and frame advance, a TV monitor, a video recorder, digital recording media, a quiet place to work, a copy of the DVD that accompanies this study set, and this book.

When and Where You Should Plan to Do the Exercises

Each exercise can be done independently. This means that you should either plan to do them out of class on your own time or in class if your educational program has a place for you to record your work. Where you do the exercises will depend on your instructor and the equipment available in your interpreter education program. For example, if your program has a language lab that will permit you to work independently and to record your work, then you can do many of the exercises independently while on campus or in class. Your teacher may introduce the exercises and go over your results with you or may provide similar exercises for you to work on in class or may use the first exercise as a group activity.

If you are a practicing interpreter and want to work on developing your skills, or work for continuing education units, you will still need all of the equipment listed previously and may proceed at your own pace. You may wish to form a study group with other interpreters in order to have a forum to discuss your skill development in analyzing both product and process.

How Many Times Should You Do the Exercises?

You can benefit from doing each exercise at least twice. When you do the exercise the first time, the material that you listen to will be "cold," or unfamiliar. The intralingual skills that you are practicing may be new and unfamiliar as well. When you do the exercise the second time, the material will be "warm," or familiar, because you have seen it once. You will be more comfortable with the process the second time. It is a good idea to practice the exercises more than once because this type of practice will allow you to experience good control of the process that you are working on and improve the quality of the process you use to create the product.

Progress Tracking Sheet

A progress tracking sheet is at the end of each unit. This sheet is designed to help you keep track of which exercises you have completed and your performance on these exercises. After completing the exercise and answering the study questions, fill in the tracking sheet. Note the date that you completed the exercise and give an indication of your level of accomplishment. You can use either a quantitative or a qualitative approach to track your progress. The sample chart that follows provides examples of how to note your progress using the quantitative or qualitative approach.

A quantitative approach uses a point scale. Assigning points to linguistic exercises is arbitrary and difficult to do. Nevertheless, in academic environments you may find the point system more common than the qualitative approach. Each of the two trials on the performance and each study question can be assigned a point value. For example, a zero indicates that the question was not answered and a 5 indicates a full and complete response. Add the scores in each column (not row) and divide by the number of exercises to get a percentage for first performance, second performance, and study questions. It is important to have separate percentages for each of these columns because the scores in the study question column represents different skills. The two performance columns measure how you actually did on the exercise. A second trial on the same material is considered practice on warm or familiar material and should be weighted less than the "cold" or first attempt.

Here is an example of a scale you can use to assign points to your work. Excellent (no serious errors) = 5 points; good (some errors, but not serious) = 4 points; fair (many errors, some serious) = 3 points; not satisfactory = 2 points (many errors, most are serious); poor =1 point (missed the point of the exercise—must redo).

A qualitative approach is well suited to those who are studying the material in an independent fashion or those who do not want to attach numbers and percentages to their work. In a qualitative approach you describe your response to your work rather than assigning numbers. Write down enough information to remind yourself of your level of achievement in the performance of the exercises and study questions.

Your teacher may ask you to photocopy this page and submit it for grading.

Exercise Number	Date	First Performance	Study Questions	Questions and Reminders	Date	Second Performance
Exercise 3.1 Quantitative	10/3	2	3		10/4	
Qualitative		Missed some fingerspelling	Complete	Review this unit		
Exercise 3.2 Quantitative	10/9	3	4		10/10	
Qualitative		Hard to follow story	Rating shows comprehension is high	Double check answers with study partner		Much improved
Exercise 3.3 Quantitative	10/15	4	5		10/16	
Qualitative				Redo all exercises so I remember		
Quantitative Totals						

UNIT
1

Main Idea
Comprehension

The interpretation process begins with comprehension. If the interpreter cannot understand the source message, the interpretation will be flawed at best. According to Taylor (2002), "Current research shows a continuing and significant gap in interpreter's ability to comprehend ASL. The ASL source message is not understood completely and thus the interpretation has no chance of being successful regardless of the interpreter processing ability" (p. 2). Taylor's research points out that most ASL interpreters are not native signers. Her research also demonstrates that there is widespread evidence for shortcomings related to ASL comprehension. " The lack of ASL comprehension that appeared regularly in the research made it clear that ASL lexicon and ASL discourse are two important features that need to be addressed in analysis and assessment (of interpretations)" (p. 7).

Comprehension underlies all of the exercises in this book. Taylor calls these basic and fundamental language skills such as comprehension "knowledge-lean" skills. This means that these skills do not depend on knowledge of the topic. In contrast, "knowledge-rich" skills refer to "context sensitive interpretation skills that allow an interpreter to communicate the subtle differences in meaning and tone that the signer is expressing" (p. 8).

The problem of ASL comprehension is made more complex according to Taylor (2002) by regional variations in signing and the variations in signing styles from person to person, ranging from ASL to signing styles that follow English syntax patterns. Taylor points out other variables that affect signing style including age, gender, type and amount of education, handedness, and whether there were other deaf members in the signer's family. One very important point that Taylor stresses is that there is no standardized approach to teaching ASL to deaf individuals and this adds to the variations we see between signers. All of these variables combine to create a situation in which interpreters must be able to comprehend a wide range of signing styles in order to be successful.

Since comprehension is central to the interpreting process, it is important to focus specific attention on comprehension practice. In this unit the emphasis is on comprehension of the most important points in an ASL selection. The careful analysis of short ASL presentations guides you in understanding the main ideas at the discourse level. Discourse level refers to the combining of words or signs into sentences or even longer segments such as paragraphs or longer texts. Direct practice in this skill for interpreters is often overlooked, which makes the development of other, more complex skills in the interpretation process difficult or impossible. This unit provides practice in finding the main idea at the discourse level and key concepts that point to the main idea.

In order to be able to identify the main idea, you must sort the ideas by level of importance and then by topic. This is accomplished using a specific type of analytical thinking called hierarchical thinking. A hierarchy is a rank ordering or arranging of things by importance.

In a well-organized speech or talk, the main idea usually is expressed early in the speech or text. The main idea can be summarized into a topic sentence. Sometimes the topic sentence is further abbreviated into a title. The main idea is stated early in the speech and then referred to again and again until the topic is changed. Once the main idea is stated, it becomes implicit or understood in the ideas that follow it. Ideas presented after the main idea can be points that clarify or support the main idea.

Topics included in this unit are as follows.

Main idea

Key word

Schema

Main Idea

In this unit the term "main idea" means the central premise around which the rest of the text is expanded. The supporting ideas are those that help expand the main idea. For interpreting, if the main idea is altered or not understood, the meaning of the text changes. The main idea contains important information. Supporting ideas add information to the main idea and make it clearer and stronger. The supporting ideas or details are less important to the overall theme than the main point. If supporting ideas are omitted, the overall main idea is not changed substantially.

You may remember reading classes in which you learned to find the main idea. The goal of finding the main idea is usually to improve or check on comprehension. Cunningham and Moore (1986) searched the literature on main idea comprehension and found that there are many terms that refer to the concept of main idea. Some of the terms associated with main idea include outstanding point, master idea, big idea, controlling idea, significant idea, and central theme. Even among professionals in the field of reading for comprehension, there is not much agreement as to how to define the main idea. Despite disagreements regarding the definition of the term, it is true that there are ideas in any passage or text that are more important than other ideas or are more central to the overall theme. Working to develop this distinction between more important and less important ideas is the goal of this unit.

Cunningham and Moore (1986) suggest that one of the factors that determine what a person selects as the main idea is what captures their attention. These authors deal primarily with finding the main idea in written materials, rather than signed, but the same principles apply to finding the main point of signed material. Cunningham and Moore say, "The reader's purposes for reading as well as writer's presentation of information serve to regulate reader's attention" (1986, p. 10). If we expand the concept of "the reader" to include the interpreter, we can see that the interpreter's purpose in attending to the ASL source message is to extract as much meaning as possible from the passage and convey it into the target language. The interpreter is not intending to gain information for his or her own personal use and so may focus more on the signer's purpose. However, as Cunningham and Moore point out, the signer's or speaker's purpose may not always be easy to find.

This skill of finding the main idea is one that is used in the real world and in interpreter education. Various authors write about the importance of this skill. Ine Van Dam (1989) describes a process she calls "Hop, Skip and Jump." By this she means that when the interpreter cannot keep up with the pace of the signer, the interpreter must hop and skip over some of the details and jump to the next main point. In order to do this, the interpreter must be able to discern which points are central and which are supporting. One way to determine which ideas are main and which are supporting is to look for key words and to consider the schema for the communicative event.

Key Word

"The key word in a passage is the one that labels the most important single concept in a passage" (Cunningham and Moore, 1986). According to Larson (1984, p.177), "Key words are used over and over in the text and are crucial to the theme or topic under discussion. Key words are most often words which represent an essential or basic concept of the text and are often thematic." Key words point to the main idea. Learning to identify key words is an effective way to improve comprehension. In this unit we adapt this idea and look for "key signs," or signs that are used over and over again to point to the main idea.

Schema

A schema is a plan or diagram. This diagram or design is usually not one that is drawn on paper but a representation in the signer's mind based on previous experience or knowledge. Signers who wish to convey information generally have a schema for that information and ideas about which parts of the information are most central to the message. This means that the signer usually has a plan for what they want to say. In addition, the concept of schema includes what the signer already knows about the topic. It can be thought of as the signer's prior history and experience with that topic. For example, a teacher giving a lecture on aerodynamics may have personal experiences with the topic as well as information obtained through study.

A schema is a pattern or a mental image about something. There can be many different schemas in any communicative event. For example, if you are a student, you have a schema for a lecture class and a different one for a lab class. Your schema for a lecture class is a mental pattern for what you expect. You have a different mental pattern for what you expect in a lab class. Schemas are usually based on real world experiences. Sometimes it is possible to create a schema for something you have never seen or experienced, but usually that schema draws on schemas for similar or related experiences that you have had before. The most important thing to realize is that schemas are very personal and no two people will have exactly the same schema, even for shared events. There is enough overlap, however, that knowing that you must tap into a schema provides a framework to organize ideas. Using this approach can improve your comprehension skills because if you try to see what frame of reference or schema the signer is using, you can better understand his or her point of view.

Each signer has his or her own schemas for the topic at hand. This crucial piece of information is usually not explicitly discussed when, and if, the signer meets with the interpreter prior to beginning the speech, meeting, or class. For example, it is unlikely that the signer will explain his or her schema to the interpreter. Rather, the signer may disclose some of the details about the content of the speech at hand and not what the signer has known about this topic and how this speech fits into the signer's overall scheme of things.

At the same time, the interpreter brings his or her own schema or frame of reference to any communicative event. Since interpreters' work often relates to varied fields of information in addition to interpretation, the frame of reference of the interpreter could possibly be the weakest of any of the participants in the communicative event. As Gile (1995) points out, interpreters rarely interpret about interpreting.

The audience member or members will also have their own frame of reference. Naturally, the interpreter cannot know all that influences the audience, but it is helpful to realize that each person brings their own frame of reference to the communicative event. Knowing that your schema may be different than the schema of the people you are working with can allow you the freedom to ask questions if you are not sure what is meant.

In this section we looked briefly at the importance of main ideas, key signs, and schemas in the interpretation process. The simultaneous interpreter must quickly grasp the important parts of the signer's message. To render a faithful interpretation, the interpreter must sort out the main ideas from the supporting ideas. This usually happens without benefit of a discussion of this organization with the signer. In the signer's mind and perhaps in the signer's written notes, some points are more important than other points. If the interpreter attributes equal weight to all of the signer's points, the message may be skewed and certainly will not match the signer's original message.

Sometimes, the signer signs very rapidly or is reading from a prepared speech. In these cases, the interpreter cannot always ask the signer to pause or repeat information. When this happens, it is important for the interpreter to select the most important points. The ideal interpretation includes all the main points and all of the supporting points, in the order originally presented. In real-world practice, this is not always possible. In situations where the interpreter is unable to slow the pace of the signer's comments, it is necessary for the interpreter to select which points are central and which are supporting.

Specific Areas of Difficulty in ASL Comprehension

Taylor's (2002) work analyzes interpreting performance with the intent of discovering patterns of miscues or errors. Once patterns are identified it is easier to develop strategies for improvement. Her research analyzed types of errors such as fingerspelled word recognition, number recognition, and ASL sign recognition, among others. In this unit we focus on these three error types.

Fingerspelled Word Recognition

Taylor notes that fingerspelled word recognition is an area where miscomprehension frequently occurs. She lists possible types of errors including omission of fingerspelled words whether the words are spelled slowly, rapidly, or in lexicalized form. The interpretation also tends to be inaccurate when the signer does not use mouth movements or uses mouth movements that do not represent Standard English pronunciation. Taylor goes on to say that "The interpreter's ability to comprehend fingerspelling has a significant impact on the effectiveness of the interpretation. If the meaning is lost or skewed because the precise meaning of the fingerspelling was not interpreted into English, then errors are present in the interpretation" (p. 34).

Patrie and Johnson (in press) point out that fingerspelled word recognition is pivotal to fully comprehending ASL because fingerspelled words are an integral part of American Sign Language. Hearing people who are learning ASL as adults tend to have great difficulty in correctly recognizing fingerspelled words. This specific difficulty often prevents hearing people from becoming truly fluent in ASL and can lead to misunderstandings and frustrations between deaf and hearing people who want to communicate with each other through the use of sign language. Problems also occur in the production of fingerspelled words, but these problems tend to be less severe than the problems of fingerspelled word recognition.

Sign language interpreters may be more acutely aware of the difficulty in correctly recognizing fingerspelled words than other hearing signers because interpretation requires simultaneously managing a wide range of enormously demanding cognitive, linguistic, and interpersonal tasks including finger-spelled word recognition. Patrie (1989) notes that many interpreters feel that the fingerspelled word recognition process is much more difficult than any other aspect of the interpretation process. When errors in fingerspelled word recognition occur, anxiety tends to increase and often the interpretation process is interrupted. These word recognition difficulties as they appear in the interpretation process mean that there are underlying deficiencies in recognition of fingerspelled words.

According to Patrie and Johnson (in press) experienced interpreters report that reading fingerspelled words is no different than reading other aspects of sign language, and that fingerspelled word recognition is not particularly anxiety producing. The successes of these interpreters must mean that they are using strategies that are appropriate to fingerspelled word recognition. In a forthcoming work by Patrie and Johnson comparisons are drawn between novice and experienced interpreters. In every comparison, the experienced interpreters performed better than the novice interpreters. One can assume that the differences in performance are due to differences in strategies. The training approaches and information presented in *Fingerspelled Word Recognition through Rapid Sequential Visual Processing* can improve strategies related to the fingerspelled word recognition process and, in turn, the overall interpretation process. These strategies include understanding the nature of the fingerspelled word, learning to rapidly process visual information, and engaging in appropriate practice techniques involving template building and practicing with fingerspelled words in context. An earlier work by Patrie (1997) developed the successful template building approach to fingerspelled word recognition.

Numbers in ASL

Taylor's research also points out that numbers in ASL are interpreted inaccurately under a variety of conditions. Errors occur when numbers are partially omitted, such as part of a year or an age. When numbers are signed rapidly the interpretation is sometimes inaccurate and conversely, when the number is signed slowly, the interpretation can also be inaccurate if the emphasis intended by the slower signing is overlooked. More complex numbering systems are another area in which errors occur. For example, when a sign indicating dollars is misunderstood as a sign indicating placement in a contest, the miscomprehension skews the message. Number incorporation, if not correctly understood, will lead to additional errors in comprehension and, thus, interpretation errors.

ASL Signs

With regard to comprehending ASL signs, Taylor notes the following types of errors. The meaning of the ASL sign is omitted, possessive pronouns are confused with nominative pronouns ("his" instead of "he"), nouns are interpreted as verbs or vice versa, noun classifications are interpreted incorrectly (APPLE-ORANGE-BANANA) is interpreted as individual lexical items rather than as "fruit." Compound signs are interpreted as individual lexical items (BLUE-SPOT) rather than "bruise," and new or regional signs are interpreted inaccurately.

By being aware of the types of errors that commonly occur in interpreting, we can focus on developing specific skills to overcome these types of common errors. The exercises that follow guide you through the process of comprehending several ASL selections. First you will identify the main ideas and then focus on a more complete comprehension of the details such as fingerspelled words and specific signs. By examining the details you will be able to confirm your understanding of the main points. Study the selections carefully, using slow motion where necessary. The goal is full comprehension of each selection.

Discussion Questions

Discuss the following questions with your students to promote insight and increase awareness of the importance of main idea comprehension as it relates to the interpretation process.

1. *How does understanding the importance of main idea identification in ASL relate to the interpretation process?*

   Interpreters must be able to quickly sift through the streams of incoming material to find the central organizing points. When the interpreter grasps which ideas are most central, then the interpreter can better sort the remaining information into details and supporting facts. This sorting helps to support strong comprehension skills because interpreters then know which points should receive greater attention.

   The ability to quickly find the "gist" is sometimes used to determine suitability for interpreter training. Finding the gist is central to the interpretation process. If the student cannot easily find the gist of the message, this may point to the fact that another profession may be a better match for that student's skills and abilities.

2. *Do you feel you have good main idea comprehension skills?*

   Ask this question before and after the drills to see if students say their skills improved and if they have greater confidence in them. Most students' comprehension skills will improve with increased focus and practice. Confidence in being able to find the main idea quickly benefits the interpreter. Rapid and reliable main idea identification drills are not automatic. These skills must be learned and practiced. Even though students think that they have accurate and reliable main idea identification skills, it is often the case that these skills need improvement.

3. *What will happen if the interpreter does not have rapid, reliable main idea identification skills?*

When the interpreter does not have quick access to main idea identification skills, then not only is the richness of the product of the interpretation compromised, but also the interpretation process is weakened. For example, the interpreter who cannot identify the main idea gets lost in the details and often misses the central point of the text.

4. *What happens when the interpreter does not know which ideas are main and which are supporting?*

    In this case the interpreter will not be able to sort out which ideas are the main ideas and will not be able to organize the supporting ideas around the main idea. When the interpreter cannot rank ideas in order of importance, all of the incoming information has the same level of importance and soon the interpreter's cognitive processing capacity will be reached or exceeded. The mind can function better if it can group relevant ideas together and distinguish ideas that are dissimilar. The result of the interpretation, in the event that the interpreter can keep going, may be a series of individually translated items without a grasp of the big picture the signer wishes to convey.

EXERCISES IN MAIN IDEA IDENTIFICATION

The following exercises are designed to provide opportunities to improve comprehension by practicing, watching, and studying naturally occurring examples of ASL. The signers on the accompanying tape chose the topics to present and did not rehearse in advance of the filming. None of the selections was scripted. In some of the study questions you will be asked to demonstrate your comprehension of fingerspelled words by repeating the fingerspelled word or by using the fingerspelled word in a sentence.

Ideally, you will have conducted the exercises in The Effective Interpreting Series: English Skills Development *before doing these corresponding exercises in ASL. Developing skills in L1 before L2 is best. Although some suggested ideas are included in written English in response to the comprehension questions, your students should respond in ASL and record their work. If students write their answers, then these are no longer intralingual exercises. However, depending on the availability of equipment and your class goals you may ask students to write responses in English. If students respond in written English it provides you with access to how much students have understood and are able to recall, but you and your students should be aware that writing answers in English is a translation exercise.*

Decide whether you want to conduct these exercises in class or whether you want the students to do these exercises on their own time. Remember that in these exercises students are encouraged to study and review the source material as often as necessary. You may want to assign students to work in teams to develop stronger support skills and promote the exchange of ideas among classmates. The first exercise is designed as a warm-up that can be done in class. You can assign the second exercise for homework and use the third as a graded exercise or for additional homework.

If you decide to conduct this exercise during class time, be sure all the students can see the TV monitor you are using. Ask the students to prepare themselves to pay careful attention. Ask all students to refrain from making noise during the time the selection is being played.

Ideally, you will guide the students through the first exercise. In Exercises 1.2 and 1.3 students should work independently. However, you can assign Exercise 2 as group work or as an out-of-class assignment. This kind of small group collaboration lays the foundation for interpreting as part of a team later.

When students do this exercise on their own, they must each have their own DVD, recording device, and recording media. If you decide to conduct this exercise during class time, be sure all the students have their own copy of the study set.

Take time to go over the directions for each section. Read the directions and explain them to the students. Allow time for questions after you have given the directions. You should plan on at least 5 minutes to prepare the students for the exercise. Five minutes should be enough if you have the group's attention and if all equipment is ready and in working order.

Possible translations/answers are provided below simply as guidance for the teacher or the interpreter studying independently. Teachers have the option of requiring written responses in addition to the ASL responses. Keep in mind that the written responses will require translation skills between ASL and English and that students may not be fully prepared to do this type of work. Written responses may be less time consuming for teachers to check. Space for written answers is provided for "get to know the signer" portions of the exercises.

EXERCISE 1.1

An Indelible Experience

ALEC NAIMAN

Directions

Student Workbook
page 21

Find this video selection on your DVD. Begin by allowing yourself time to focus on the signer's face and begin to concentrate. The first clip is about one minute long and allows you to get to know the signer. Watch the entire selection once. Answer as many questions as you can using ASL. Watch the entire first selection again, pausing the DVD to study any portion you do not fully understand. Play the second clip which is about two minutes long. Review it until you can answer the study questions in ASL. You will need a video recorder for this exercise. You should respond in ASL but your teacher may also require responses in written English in the spaces provided.

Get to Know the Signer

This short segment allows you to get acquainted with the signer. Watch the selection and replay it until you can answer the following questions in ASL.

1. What is the signer's name? Play the tape in slow motion as many times as you need to in order to understand the name. How many times did it take?

    Alec Naiman

    _____

2. Where was the signer born?

    Atlanta, Georgia

    _____

3. How old was he when he moved to New York?

    When he was 9 years old his family moved to NYC.

    _____

4. What was the name of the school he attended in NYC?

    Lexington

    _____

5. What does this sign mean?

       01:00:40;20

    Traveled around the world

    _____

6. How long did he travel around the world?

    4 1/2 years

_____

7. Where did he go to college and what was his major? What were his minors?

    NYU, Anthropology, German and Physics

_____

Study Questions

Video record your answers for the following questions in ASL using complete sentences. Your responses should demonstrate that you know what the sign means in this context.

1. What does this sign mean in this context?

    01:01:36;09

    An indelible memory

2. What does this sign mean in this context?

    01:01:39;29

    Thailand

3.   What does this sign mean in this context?

01:01:47;21

Viet Nam

4.   Identify this fingerspelled word and use it in a sentence.

01:01:51;04

River

5.   Describe the boat and the location of the people in the boat.

It was a long narrow boat with a motor in the rear. A man was seated in the front and Alec was seated behind him.

6.   What was the nationality of the man in the front of the boat and what was his job?

He was a Thai man who worked for the U. S. Drug Enforcement Agency.

7.   What kind of gun did the other man in the boat have?

He had a Colt 45.

8.   What was the other man shooting at and what effect did it have on Alec?

The Thai man was shooting at an animal and the bullet passed right over Alec's head. After that experience Alec had a deep dislike of guns.

9. What is the main idea of this selection? Record a single sentence in ASL that captures the overall idea of the passage.

    The signer provides a brief description of an event that happened in Thailand that led to his dislike of guns.

10. If you try to see what frame of reference or schema the signer is using, you can better understand their point of view. What do you think the signer's schema is for this topic?

    He lived through the experience he is describing and is using his knowledge of the event to describe it.

11. Record yourself providing more details about the passage. Provide the details in the order in which they occurred in the selection.

EXERCISE 1.2

My Goal
QUINTIN GREENFIELD

Directions

Student Workbook
page 25

Find this video selection on your DVD. Begin by allowing yourself time to focus on the signer's face and begin to concentrate. This video selection is about 3 minutes long. Watch the entire selection once. Record your answers to as many study questions as you can. Watch the entire selection again, stopping the video to study any portion you do not fully understand. Answer any remaining study questions. You will need a video recorder for this exercise. Your responses should be in ASL but your teacher may also require responses in written English.

Study Questions

1. What is the main idea of this selection? Record a single sentence in ASL that captures the overall idea of the passage.

    The signer provides a brief overview of how he became involved in deaf blind interpreting.

2. What key word does the signer use to point to the main idea? What do you think the signer's schema is for this topic?

    Deaf blind

    He has experience with deaf blind people and interpreting for them.

3. Record yourself providing more detail about the passage. Provide the details in the order in which they occurred in the selection.

4. What is the signer's name? Play the tape in slow motion as many times as you need to in order to understand the name. How many times did it take? Respond in ASL.

    Quintin Greenfield

5. Which person in the couple was deaf blind?

    The wife.

6. What does this sign mean in this context ? Explain in ASL.

    01:03:10;29

    For this particular situation in communicating with a deaf blind person, I was not sure what to do.

7. What does this sign mean in this context? Explain in ASL.

    01:03:22;10

    That was amazing. Wow, I couldn't believe it.

8. What does this sign refer to in this context? Explain in ASL.

01:03:24;28

He expected the deaf blind person's hands to be heavy on his hands.

9. What does this sign mean in this context? Explain in ASL.

01:03:28;29

Oh great! WOW!

10. How old was the person when the blindness started?

01:03:39;15

She was 21 when she started having decreased vision.

11. What does this sign mean in this context? Explain in ASL.

01:03:41;27

Usher's Syndrome

12. What does this sign mean in this context? Explain in ASL.

01:03:46;03

Oh, so that is how it is.

13. What does this sign mean in this context? Explain in ASL.

01:03:53;18

Met many people

14. What is the sign for this fingerspelled word?

01:04:08;28

GLASSES

15. Repeat this fingerspelled name.

01:04:25;18

Steve Collins

16. What does this sign mean in this context?

01:04:38;08

Blind people

17. Repeat this fingerspelled word.

01:04:50;23

Mark

18. What is the purpose of marking an "X" on the person's back?

To let them know that they must allow a guide to lead them to a safer place.

19. What do these signs mean in this context? Explain in ASL.

01:05:25;25 to 01:05:27;02

This idea relates back to a previously learned point.

EXERCISE 1.3

Hot Peppers

BARBARA BUCHANAN

Directions

Student Workbook
page 29

Find this video selection on your DVD. Begin by allowing yourself time to focus on the signer's face and begin to concentrate. The first clip is about one minute long and allows you to get to know the signer. Watch the entire selection once. Answer as many questions as you can using ASL. Watch the entire first clip again, pausing the DVD to study any portion you do not fully understand until you have answered all of the questions about the signer. Play the second clip, which is about five minutes long. Review it until you can answer the study questions in ASL. You will need a video recorder for this exercise. You should respond in ASL but your teacher may also require responses in written English in the spaces provided.

Get to Know the Signer

This short segment allows you to get acquainted with the signer. Watch the selection and replay it until you can answer the following questions in ASL.

1. What is the signer's name? Play the DVD in slow motion as many times as you need to in order to understand the name. How many times did it take?

    Barbara Buchanan

    _____

2. Where does she live? Where was she raised? At what age did she become deaf?

    San Diego, North Carolina, age 5.

    _____

Study Questions

1. What does this sign mean in this context?

01:06:41;23

Moved to San Diego

2. What is the signer referring to in the space to her left? Respond in ASL.

01:06:42;27

San Diego

3. When did she move? What kinds of plants were left in her friend's garden?

1983, various kinds of peppers including jalapeños

4. What does this sign mean in this context? Respond in ASL.

01:07:13;18

Waste

5. What does this sign mean in this context? Respond in ASL.

01:07:18;22

Gather

6. What is the signer referring to in this frame? Respond in ASL.

01:07:25;03

Adding peppers to chili.

7. What is the signer moving to her right in this frame? Respond in ASL.

01:07:38;02

She is moving the peppers that have been washed and patted dry.

8. Repeat the fingerspelled word and use it in a sentence.

01:07:44;26

Stem

9. What does this sign mean in this context? Respond in ASL.

01:07:51;04

Remove the seeds

10. Repeat the fingerspelled word and use it in a sentence.

01:07:52;07

Seeds

11. Repeat the fingerspelled word and use it in a sentence.

01:07:55;25

Bag

12. What does this sign mean in this context? Respond in ASL.

01:08:10;01

Burning, on fire.

13. Describe in ASL the meaning of this facial expression and this sign.

01:08:18;20

The sign referred to here is glossed as SILLY and could be translated as 'oh gosh' 'gee, that hurt.'

14. What did she wash her hands with? Did washing her hands stop the burning?

Soap and a brush. No, the burning got worse.

15. This sign is repeated several times and is done with two hands. Contrast the meaning of this sign with the sign referred to in question 13.

01:08:40;00

The pain was really approaching unbearable now.

16. What helped reduce the burning? How long did she keep her hands there?

    Putting her hands in a bowl of ice water helped. An hour.

17. What does this sign mean in this context? Explain in ASL.

01:09:08;15

I didn't feel like keeping my hands in ice any more.
I had enough of keeping my hands in the ice.

18. What did she try next? Did it help?

    She used lotion. It made it burn again.

19. Who is the signer talking to here and what was that person's response? Explain in ASL.

01:09:25;18

Her friend. Her friend did not know what to do either.

20. Who did she ask her friend to phone? What happened to her fingertips?

    Urgent care facility. Her fingertips started to look like raisins.

21. What did her friend suggest that Barbara put on her hands?

    Meat tenderizer.

22. Describe how she slept to keep her hands from burning.

She put her hands over her head and soaked them in a bowl of ice water at the end of the bed.

23. What will she do if she decides to cut peppers in the future?

She will use rubber gloves.

Watch each of the selections in this unit again and mentally note when the signer states one of the important points and when she states supporting points. Make a mental outline of these points as a way to practice sorting and ranking ideas as you watch them.

You can suggest other materials for students to practice ranking and organizing ideas. For example, selections from other exercises in this study set and DVD are appropriate for comprehension exercises.

Progress Tracking Sheet

Use this sheet to track your progress with the exercises you have completed. After performing the exercise (one or two times) and answering the study questions, fill in the tracking sheet. Note the date that you completed the exercise and give an indication of your level of accomplishment. You can use either a quantitative or a qualitative approach to track your progress.

Exercise Number	Date	First Performance	Study Questions	Questions and Reminders	Date	Second Performance
Exercise 1.1 Quantitative						
Qualitative						
Exercise 1.2 Quantitative						
Qualitative						
Exercise 1.3 Quantitative						
Qualitative						
Quantitative Totals						

UNIT
2

Summarizing

Strong comprehension skills underlie the ability to summarize. In this unit we continue our focus on developing strong comprehension skills. As Peterson (2002) points out, comprehension should precede expression in learning a language. However, in many cases interpreting students have not had sufficient practice in developing comprehension before being expected to use expressive skills in ASL. As Peterson suggests, one cannot expect that comprehension is a byproduct of learning to sign. Instead, we must use specific techniques to improve comprehension. Peterson suggests that deductive reasoning can help us figure out the meaning of a sign we do not know if we understand the information and context surrounding that sign. This is described by Peterson (and others) as *top down processing or macro processing*.

One of the abilities central to the interpretation process is summarizing or capturing the gist of the selection. According to Tommola (1995), summarizing is so important that it is often used as an aptitude test for candidates entering interpretation programs. Tommola says, "Among the various characteristics that interpreter aptitude tests attempt to measure, a central one is the ability to analyze the source message into its semantic elements, to create a representation of the content, and to retain this representation in memory so that it can be rendered in the target language" (p. 471). Tommola goes on to suggest that being able to do *macro* processing, or finding main ideas and being aware of the relationships between them, demonstrates less effort used for processing ,which is desirable for interpreters. "This process [macro processing] includes the restructuring of incoming information into more abstract units of meaning which subsume the lower-level details." Retrieval of the hierarchically stored abstract units is an essential aspect of consecutive and, to some extent, simultaneous interpreting. The processes described by Tommola are central to summarizing.

The opposite of top-down or macro processing is bottom-up processing. According to Peterson (2002), bottom-up processing starts at the word or lexical level and combines information into larger and larger units. He explains that new signers often get stuck when trying to attach an English word to an ASL sign, especially when no one-to-one correspondence exists. Interpreters probably use both types, top-down and bottom-up, simultaneously and without real awareness of which type they are using. Using both types is generally called *interactive processing*. Because the interactive approach provides a variety of complementary strategies, it is an effective way to practice. The exercises in this unit are designed to develop an interactive processing approach to comprehension by guiding your attention through many of the details and then asking you to provide a summary. A clear and accurate summary implies that all of the details have been fully understood and the main points have been selected and organized into a concise, shorter version of the longer text.

The Role of Summarizing

Being able to recall the gist of the information presented leads to finding the rest of the relevant information in memory. An accurate and concise summary can "trigger" other related details in your memory. This kind of trigger may last only a short time, since interpreters generally are not trying to create long-term memories based on what they saw. Rather, they are relying heavily on working memory to process what they are seeing while they are continuing to interpret.

During the interpretation process, there is a constant sorting of information. The interpreter must determine which information is very important or less important. The interpreter makes this decision based on their schema, what they know about the topic, and what they know about the audience. The interpreter also constantly sorts information into categories or topics. For the exercises in this unit this constant sorting process will allow you to know which points are most important and should be included in your summaries.

Analysis of the Target Audience

While being able to provide a quick and accurate summary is a desirable skill for an interpreter to have, there are many questions that must be considered before the summary is created. The target audience must be evaluated in terms of their composition and information needs. In addition to the actual content and arrangement of the linguistic information, cultural information must be considered. If the summary is created without regard to audience needs and cultural information, then the summary will not be as accurate or relevant as it could be.

Although intralingual exercises don't require audience analysis, the audience an interpreter is working to is ordinarily studied in relation to the skill of simultaneous interpreting. It is presented here because this type of analysis takes time to develop and should be introduced early in interpretation study as a critically important feature.

Below is a list of factors that can affect audience composition. A selection from among these can create hypothetical audiences for you to "face." Based on the hypothetical audience composition, you can strengthen your reasoning for how you present the summarized information.

- Size

  Large — over 50 people
  Medium — 25 to 49 people
  Small — under 25 people
  Interview setting — 3 or 4 participants

- Language used by the audience members and which register of that language is most appropriate for the setting and participants

- Hearing status of the group members. This variable is important for signed language interpreters regardless of which type of signed language is used

  All deaf members
  All hearing members
  Mix of hearing and deaf
  Unknown — i.e., sometimes you do not know whether there are any deaf people or whether there are any hearing people in the audience

- Background knowledge of the group

  Knowledgeable about a topic, i.e., a special conference on the topic, and we assume those in attendance know the jargon and related background information

Cultural Information

Cultural information cannot be separated from linguistic information. For example, if a speech is about Telecommunications Devices for the Deaf usage, and if the speech is being given to hearing people who do not have prior experience with the deaf community, a summary of the information would reflect this information. Sometimes it is not possible for the interpreter to know the composition of the audience and their prior collective knowledge. However, as an exercise, it is valuable to describe the audience so that you can use inference skills and then determine what the main points are and whether they should be phrased with less or more detail.

It will not always be possible to answer all the questions raised in this chapter before beginning a summary or an interpretation. There may be other more relevant variables in addition to the ones mentioned here. Nevertheless, you can be aware that there may be unanswered questions and in that case, you proceed to make decisions based on what can be observed, plus what can be inferred from those observations. When working from inference, you must be ready to change to a different set of assumptions as information builds during the interpreting assignment.

Summarization skills are valuable for the interpreter in training as well as for the working interpreter. Summarization skills show that you can get the "big picture" of what the speech is about, and exhibits that strong comprehension skills are in place. A strong summary depends on fully understanding all the details, of the speech, the context in which the selection is situated, and the potential audience for the summary.

Discussion Questions

Discuss the following questions with your students to promote insight and increase awareness of the importance of developing summarization skills.

1. *How do summary skills in ASL relate to the interpretation process?*

   Creating a short summary may also be thought of as finding the gist of a passage. A summary can be a single sentence or a short paragraph. The ability to find the gist of a passage is often used as a predictor for interpretation skills. The presence of this ability shows that the interpreter is able to find the central organizing principle of the talk or text.

2. *Do you feel your summary of a text would be exactly the same as another person's summary?*

   Each person's summary may be slightly different in form but the meaning should be approximately the same. In other words, it should be possible for two people to agree on the most important points in a given text, even though they use different words to express the ideas.

3. *What happens when two people do not agree on what points are most important in a given passage or text?*

   Based on prior experiences, each person brings different perceptual information to each communicative event. Due to this difference in perceptual background information, it is possible that two people might not agree on what is most important. For an interpreter, it is even more important to be able to find the central organizing principles of a talk or text. The interpreter must be aware that there are various ways to see and understand things. When the interpreter can see several possible viewpoints, it is important for the interpreter to ask the signer for clarification.

4. *What do you think will happen if the interpreter does not know how to create a succinct summary?*

The inability to make a quick and concise summary may not show up in every-day interpreting. However, the interpreter who can demonstrate a quick grasp of the material at hand is more likely to be able to render a faithful interpretation than an interpreter who is unable to sort out unimportant from important points.

SUMMARIZING EXERCISES

EXERCISE 2.1

Dad's Car
ELIZABETH CREAMER

Directions

Student Workbook page 40

Find this video selection on your DVD. Begin by allowing yourself time to focus on the signer's face and begin to concentrate. The first clip is about one minute long and allows you to get to know the signer. Watch the entire selection once. Answer as many questions as you can using ASL. Watch the entire selection again, pausing the DVD to study any portion you do not fully understand. Play the second clip, which is about six minutes long. Review it until you can complete the study questions in ASL. You will need a video recorder for this exercise. You should respond in ASL but your teacher may also require responses in written English in the spaces provided.

Get to Know the Signer

This short segment allows you to get acquainted with the signer. Watch the selection and replay it until you can answer the following questions in ASL.

1. What is the signer's name?

   Elizabeth Creamer

   _____

2. Where is she from?

   Philadelphia, Pennsylvania

   _____

3. How many generations of deafness in her family?

   Three

   _____

4. How many deaf siblings are there?

   Three

   _____

5. What is her current job?

   Faculty member in the department of social work at Gallaudet University.

   _____

Study Questions

1. Describe the audience for which you are creating a summary.

   _____

2. What does this sign mean in this context? Video record your ASL response. Do not use the sign in your explanation.

   01:12:19;22

Incredible, awful

3. What does this sign mean in this context? Video record your ASL response.

01:12:25;24

Time. Here it means "at that time" and does not refer to clock time.

4. Where did she go to exercise and what did she do when she got there?

She went to the park and ran laps around the football field.

5. What does this sign mean in this context? Video record your ASL response.

01:13:38;20

Oh good, you are here. Perfect, now you are here.

6. Look at this segment and find the frames that show the sign "FATHER" (01:13:37;28) and the sign for the pronoun referring to the signer herself (01:13:44;15). Why does the signer switch from signing with her left hand to signing with her right hand?

'FATHER' is indicated at 01:13:37;28

Pronoun for 'I' is indicated at 01:13:44;15

The signer switches to her right hand when her father starts speaking. Eye gaze also indicates a different signer. Also, it is not likely that the 17 yr old would own a car or ask herself to move it.

7. What does this sign mean in this context? Video record your ASL response.

01:13:40;20

Would you? Would you mind doing this for me?

8. Study this section to see how she gets in the car, shuts the door and puts the car in gear. Be sure you fully understand each sign and how it is used. Record yourself repeating this part of the selection to demonstrate your comprehension.

01:13:52;22 to 01:13:56;21

9. What does this sign mean in this context? Video record your ASL response.

01:14:06;00

Wanted to make the most of the opportunity to drive

10. What does this sign mean in this context? Video record your ASL response.

01:14:30;19

She drove her father's car into the back of a parked car in front of her.

11. What does this sign mean in this context? Video record your ASL response.

01:14:38;08

Would Dad bawl me out?

12. Describe what happened after she came to the third turn.

First she hit the car in front of her, and then she backed into a car behind her.

13. How much damage was done to her father's car?

Just a few scratches.

14. Describe in ASL what happened when the policeman came to her car. Show both Elizabeth and the policeman's part of the dialogue in your answer.

The policeman spoke to her but she could not understand him. He gestured that he wanted her license but she did not have it with her. He agreed to follow her to her home.

15. How far from home was she when she had the two fender benders? Respond using a full sentence in ASL.

    She was two blocks from home.

16. What does this sign mean in this context?

01:16:22;26

    I was really sweating it.

17. What does this sign mean in this context?

01:16:36;04

    Oh yeah. Whoo hoo.

18. Why didn't she have her license with her?

    She had just returned from exercising in the park and had not had a chance to go in the house to get it.

19. What did the policeman tell her father to do in the future?

    Make sure his daughter had her license and registration with her at all times when driving.

20. Review the selection again and notice how the signer marks the sentence boundaries. This signer usually closes her eyes or looks down. Her hands may move to neutral space. Note how these variables change when she starts a new sentence. What is the time code for the end of a sentence in this selection?

For extra practice, you can ask students to watch the entire selection and write the timecode corresponding to the end of each sentence.

Example: Marks the end of the sentence.

01:12:21;16

_____

_____

21. Do you have a schema for driving a car? Do you remember how you felt when you learned how to drive? How did having a schema for learning to drive help you to understand this passage? Respond in ASL and record your work.

22. Record an ASL summary of this selection. The paragraph should contain four or five sentences and should be well organized. Practice your summary in advance of recording it.

Optional Exercise

Exchange the video of your summary paragraph that you think is most accurate with a classmate or colleague and list the main points in each other's summary. Are the main points the same?

Differences can lead to class discussions regarding which information must be included in a good summary.

Directions

Student Workbook
page 46

EXERCISE 2.2

Embarrassing Moment
STEVE SANDY

Find this video selection on your DVD. Begin by allowing yourself time to focus on the signer's face and begin to concentrate. The first clip is about one minute long and allows you to get to know the signer. Watch the entire selection once. Answer as many questions as you can using ASL. Watch the entire first clip again, pausing the DVD to study any portion you do not fully understand until you have answered all of the questions about the signer. Play the second clip, which is about three minutes long. Review it until you can complete the study questions in ASL. You will need a video recorder for this exercise.

Get to Know the Signer

This short segment allows you to get acquainted with the signer. Watch the selection and replay it until you can answer the following questions in ASL.

1. What is the signer's name?

    Steve Sandy

    _____

2. What is the cause of his deafness? Does he have deaf family members?

    The cause of his deafness is unknown. No.

    _____

3. Has he traveled all the way around the world?

    No.

    _____

4. Where was he born? Where has he lived?

Hawaii. Many places, including Alaska, Hawaii, Alabama, Spain, Washington, DC, Pennsylvania.

Study Questions

1. Describe the audience for which you are creating a summary.

---

2. What type of schools did he attend? Which school did he like best?

Mainstream, residential school for the deaf, public school. Residential school for the deaf.

3. Why has he seen so much of the world?

His father was in the Air Force.

4. Where did his most embarrassing moment occur?

On a flight from Madrid to New York.

5. What is the sign that can be used to express the fingerspelled word that begins at this timecode?

01:19:24;07

LATE

01:19:25;15

Note: Lexicalized version of B-A-C-K.

6. What kind of airplane was it?

01:19:27;25

Military

7. Why did he have difficulty getting a flight?
    The military plane was fully booked.

8. Which airline did he fly?
    TWA

9. Where did he get on the plane?
    Madrid

10. Why was he concerned?
    He knew his girlfriend was waiting and that he would be late.

11. What did he do to ease his distress?
    He paced the aisles in the plane.

12. What was the nationality of the man who spoke to him?

    Arab

13. What did the man ask Steve?

    Are you going to Oklahoma?

14. Where did Steve say he was going?

    Washington, DC

15. Where did the man sit and how did they communicate?

    The man sat next to him in a vacant seat and they communicated through writing.

16. Why did the man ask if Steve was going to Oklahoma?

    Because Steve looked like a cowboy pacing around the plane.

17. What was Steve's reaction to that idea?

    He said to himself that he was an Easterner, but thought it was funny that he was perceived as a cowboy.

18. Record an ASL summary of this selection. The paragraph should contain four or five sentences and should be well organized.

EXERCISE 2.3

Turning Points

MARK MORALES

Directions

Student Workbook
page 49

Find this video selection on your DVD. Begin by allowing yourself time to focus on the signer's face and begin to concentrate. The first clip is about one minute long and allows you to get to know the signer. Watch the entire selection once. Answer as many questions as you can using ASL. Watch the entire first clip again, pausing the DVD to study any portion you do not fully understand until you have answered all of the questions about the signer. Play the second clip, which is about four minutes long. Review it until you can complete the study questions in ASL. You will need a video recorder for this exercise.

Get to Know the Signer

This short segment allows you to get acquainted with the signer. Watch the selection and replay it until you can answer the following questions in ASL.

1. What is the signer's name?

   Mark Morales

   _____

2. How many people in his family are deaf?

   Just one, Mark himself.

   _____

3. Did he use sign language while growing up?

   No, he was raised orally.

   _____

4. How many deaf students were in his high school class?

   Forty

   _____

5. Where is he from?

   La Punte near Los Angeles, California

   _____

6. When did he arrive at Gallaudet?

   1979

   _____

7. What happened when he arrived at Gallaudet?

   He was in culture shock to see so many people signing.

   _____

8. Where does he work now?

At Gallaudet University

_____

Study Questions

1. Describe the audience for which you are creating a summary in the space provided.

    _____

    _____

2. In what country and city did this turning point take place?

    Russia, Moscow

3. What was the name of the group he was traveling with?

    Discovery staff

4. What sign does he use for Moscow?

01:24:18;00

5. In what year?

    1991

6. Who was the workshop for?

    Hearing teachers, psychologists, and professors.

7. Who invited him to visit outside of Moscow?

01:24:46;21

Deaf friends from Russia.

8. What were conditions like for the people they visited outside of Moscow?

    The conditions were very poor and the buildings were ramshackle.

9. Describe the conditions at the friend's house. What is the Russian word for house?

    There was barely enough electricity, there was not much food, no coffee and limited portions of everything.

    Dacha

10. What are the fingerspelled words between **01:25:42;15** to **01:25:48;27**.

01:25:42;15

Outdoor, parks.

11. How long did he stay in Moscow?

    Three weeks

12. What does this sign mean in this context?

01:26:26;23

Russian people had nothing at all.

13. What does this sign mean in this context?

01:26:28;27

Shocked me. Brought me up short. Made me realize.

14. How did the experience change him?

    After the trip he decided to be there for people, regardless of their nationality, and to realize that all human beings are a family.

15. Record an ASL summary of this selection. The paragraph should contain four or five sentences and should be well organized.

Progress Tracking Sheet

Use this sheet to track your progress with the exercises you have completed. After performing the exercise (one or two times) and answering the study questions, fill in the tracking sheet. Note the date that you completed the exercise and give an indication of your level of accomplishment. You can use either a quantitative or a qualitative approach to track your progress.

Exercise Number	Date	First Performance	Study Questions	Questions and Reminders	Date	Second Performance
Exercise 2.1 Quantitative						
Qualitative						
Exercise 2.2 Quantitative						
Qualitative						
Exercise 2.3 Quantitative						
Qualitative						
Quantitative Totals						

UNIT

3

Lexical Substitution

Lexical substitution is the process of replacing a sign or lexical item with another sign or lexical item while keeping the meaning of the message as constant as possible. Naturally, the meaning will not be exactly the same if you replace a word or sign. In some cases a single sign can be replaced by a phrase, or vice versa, as long as the meaning remains as close to the original as possible. The ability to replace specific lexical items is a foundational skill. We know from recent research that difficulties with foundational skills can lead to faulty interpretations. Taylor's (2002) research focused on developing a diagnostic assessment instrument to evaluate ASL to English interpretations. Her goal was to determine what patterns of behavior were demonstrated by successful interpreters. Her work describes the types of errors that can occur when foundational skills, such as those at the lexical level, are absent. This unit focuses on one of the skills mentioned by Taylor, developing skill and flexibility within the ASL lexicon.

Specific Words to General Words

Before moving into exercises in ASL it is important to understand some of the general principles that underlie substitution drills. It is useful to develop lexical substitution because there will be times during the interpretation process when the exact sign does not come to mind. When that happens, using a more general term can preserve the meaning and allow the interpretation to continue. Lexical substitution is important in translation and interpretation for another reason. Since words in the source language do not necessarily have a one-to-one correspondence with words in various target languages, it is important to be able to select the word that comes closest in meaning in the target language to the word used in the source language. When the interpreter has a large vocabulary and is able to analyze the linguistic and social context in which the message is situated, then the interpreter is more likely to render an interpretation that is faithful to the original message. The linguistic context lets us know important things like whether the message is situated in a speech or conversation and what languages and cultures are involved, among other things. The social context is made up of the setting, such as a formal meeting or a hospital setting, and the people who are in the communicative event.

The Role of Lexical Substitution

Developing lexical substitution skills increases linguistic flexibility. The ability to quickly find an alternate way of expressing an idea is one of the component skills required in the simultaneous interpretation process. Being able to access a large vocabulary without hesitation is very important. The more sure you are about a wide range of signs and their meanings, the better.

If you realize that a single sign can contain an entire concept, it will be easier for you to correctly interpret. For example, if you know that the sign "MOTHER" has several concepts within it (female, has one or more children, etc.) you will be better able to understand the term itself and to find acceptable alternate lexical expressions, if necessary. Another example of how lexical substitution skills can improve linguistic flexibility in the interpretation process is that in the event that the desired lexical item cannot be retrieved from memory, a description of what that sign means might suffice.

In some cases it will be necessary to express the concept in a more formal way or in a more informal way than expressed in the original concept. These kinds of changes are called changes in register and can often be accomplished by lexical substitution. For example, the source language may be "The man gave a talk." If the target language had no equivalents in this fairly informal register, it might be necessary to say "The professor gave a lecture." In this case the higher register words are also more specific than the words used in the original. Register variation occurs in all languages.

Practicing lexical substitution is one way to increase linguistic flexibility. In order to have rapid and effective lexical substitution skills you must devote some time to specific practice. The exercise in this unit will help you develop awareness and skill in substitution at the lexical level.

Discussion Questions

Raise the following questions with your students to promote discussion and increase awareness of the importance of lexical substitution skills as they relate to the interpretation process.

1. *How does an understanding of the lexical substitution process in ASL relate to the interpretation process?*

   Lexical substitution drills can increase the range of lexical items quickly available for the interpreter to use. Since the simultaneous interpretation process is so cognitively demanding, it is important to reduce cognitive effort wherever possible. One way to help reduce the effort needed is to practice the many tasks that make up the interpretation process. One of the relevant skills is lexical substitution. Be sure to point out that it is necessary to practice this skill within each of the languages in the interpretation process. Some students may feel that if ASL is their first language they do not need to study ASL during their interpretation studies. However, most students, whether ASL is their first language or not, have not had the opportunity to practice ASL substitution drills. This skill can provide great linguistic flexibility for the interpreter.

2. *Do you feel you have good lexical substitution skills?*

   Ask this question before and after the drills and see whether students feel their skills have improved and whether they have greater confidence in them. Most students will improve with increased focus and practice. Confidence in being able to find the necessary words quickly is beneficial to the interpreter. Rapid and reliable lexical substitution drills are not automatic. These skills must be learned and practiced. This question is designed to improve awareness of skill level before and after the exercises.

3. *What will happen if the interpreter does not have rapid, reliable lexical substitution skills?*

   When the interpreter does not have quick access to various ways to express the same concept, then the richness of the product is compromised. For example, if an interpreter is working from English to ASL and only knows one translation of a particular sign, the interpreter's work into ASL will be limited in scope and register.

4. *What happens when the interpreter does not know the meaning of the word that must be substituted?*

   If the interpreter does not understand the word, then he or she cannot find an appropriate substitute. This weakness indicates a need for greater vocabulary development.

EXERCISES IN LEXICAL SUBSTITUTION

This unit provides exercises in lexical substitution. In doing the exercises, you will be working from video material, but you may pause the DVD to provide your answers. You will respond in ASL and record your work.

Read the directions and explain them to the students. Allow time for questions after you have given the directions. You should plan on at least 5 minutes to prepare the students for the exercise. Five minutes should be enough if you have the group's attention and if all students have their study sets ready.

Decide whether you want to conduct this exercise in class or if you want the students to do this exercise on their own time. In either case, each student must have his or her own study set. The exercises in this unit can be done in a group setting. Students respond by videotaping their responses. Some suggested responses are provided, although you will find other answers acceptable. Keep in mind that these answers are English translations, not glosses. For questions that ask for substitutions, the suggested answers are English translations of an alternate ASL sign or phrase not an exact translation of the ASL in the clip.

EXERCISE 3.1

Pacific Beach Incident

MATT ELLIS

Directions

Student Workbook
page 57

Find this video selection on your DVD. Begin by allowing yourself time to focus on the signer's face and begin to concentrate. The first clip is about one minute long and allows you to get to know the signer. Watch the entire selection once. Answer as many questions as you can using ASL. Watch the entire first clip again, pausing the DVD to study any portion you do not fully understand until you have answered all of the questions about the signer. Watch the second clip. Make sure you fully understand the entire selection before answering the study questions. Watch it again, if necessary. Answer each study question in the following manner. Record the original sign (indicated for you in the video captures) as exactly as possible. Watch the signer carefully. Record the sign or signs you will use to replace the original sign. Lexical substitution exercises increase your linguistic flexibility and mirroring the signing of a native signer increases your fluency.

Get to Know the Signer

This short segment allows you to get acquainted with the signer. Watch the selection and replay it until you can answer the following questions in ASL.

1. Where was he born and raised?

   California

   _____

2. Where does he work?

   DawnSignPress

   _____

Study Questions

1. Comprehension of context

   a. Where does the story take place?

   The bay at Pacific Beach in San Diego

   b. Which skill did he want to improve?

   Paddling

2. Replace these two signs with another sign or signs that preserve the meaning as closely as possible.

01:27:48;21 to 01:27:49;25

Experienced, got around in the water just fine

Knew how to go out in the water and come back

The friend was an "old pro" at paddling.

3. Replace these two signs with another sign or signs that preserve the meaning as closely as possible.

01:27:49;29 to **01:27:50;25**

No problem

Without difficulty

Easily

4. Replace these signs with another sign or signs that preserve the meaning as closely as possible.

01:27:50;27 to **01:27:52;11**

Really? Good.

My friend never had a problem at the bay, so we went ahead.

5. Who is the signer referring to with this sign? What other signs can you use to express this idea? Note that this pronoun makes it clear who the signer is referring to in the sentence that follows.

01:27:52;11

My friend

6. Replace these signs with another sign or signs that preserve the meaning as closely as possible.

01:27:52;25 to 01:27:55;00

Watched and commented on my paddling

7. Who is the signer referring to in using this sign?

01:27:55;03

He is referring to himself. It is important to notice when the signer has used a pronoun so that you know who he is referring to now.

8. How else can you express this idea?

01:27:55;17

Make changes

9. Replace this sign with another sign or signs that preserve the meaning as closely as possible.

01:27:57;10

Very far out

10. Replace this signs with another sign or signs that preserve the meaning as closely as possible.

01:27:58;19

We paddled next to each other but my friend was ahead of me.

11. Replace these signs with another sign or signs that preserve the meaning as closely as possible.

01:28:01;17

I paddled as hard as I could.

12. Replace this sign with another sign or signs that preserve the meaning as closely as possible.

01:28:04;06

Very far

So far I couldn't see him

13. Replace this sign with another sign or signs that preserve the meaning as closely as possible.

01:28:06;13

Maybe

I suppose

Approximately

14. Replace this sign with another sign or signs that preserve the meaning as closely as possible.

01:28:10;05

Exhausted

Very tired

15. Replace this sign with another sign or signs that preserve the meaning as closely as possible.

01:28:12;14

Turned around

Turned my surfboard around

16. Replace this sign with another sign or signs that preserve the meaning as closely as possible.

01:28:16;05

Paddled rapidly back to shore

Went right by me back to the beach

Note: Pronoun at **01:28:18;06** shows that now the signer is referring to himself.

17. Replace this sign with another sign or signs that preserve the meaning as closely as possible.

01:28:21;05

Muscles cramped

18. Replace this sign with another sign or signs that preserve the meaning as closely as possible.

01:28:25;13

People walking on the boardwalk

19. Replace this sign with another sign or signs that preserve the meaning as closely as possible.

01:28:34;05

Had an idea

Had a gut feeling

Sensed something

20. Replace these signs with another sign or signs that preserve the meaning as closely as possible.

01:28:41;29 to 01:28:44;20

Driver was not looking

21. Replace this with another sign or signs that preserve the meaning as closely as possible.

01:28:46;17

The driver was shocked to see me in front of him.

22. Replace this sign with another sign or signs that preserve the meaning as closely as possible.

01:28:54;07

Ducked under the surfboard

23. Replace this fingerspelled word with a sign that preserves the meaning as closely as possible.

01:28:58;11

Board

24. How much time did he have to react?

One-tenth of a second

25. Replace this sign with a sign or signs that preserves the meaning as closely as possible.

01:29:19;17

Never forget

Always remember

Directions

Student Workbook
page 65

EXERCISE 3.2

Memory of Grandfather
DONNETTE PATTERSON

Find this video selection on your DVD. Begin by allowing yourself time to focus on the signer's face and begin to concentrate. The first clip is about one minute long and allows you to get to know the signer. Watch the entire selection once. Answer as many questions as you can using ASL. Watch the entire first clip again, pausing the DVD to study any portion you do not fully understand until you have answered all of the questions about the signer. Watch the second clip. Make sure you fully understand the entire selection before answering the study questions. Watch it again, if necessary. Answer each study question in the following manner. Record the original sign (indicated for you in the video captures) as exactly as possible. Watch the signer carefully. Record the sign or signs you will use to replace the original sign. Lexical substitution exercises increase your linguistic flexibility and mirroring the signing of a native signer increases your fluency.

Get to Know the Signer

This short segment allows you to get acquainted with the signer. Watch the selection and replay it until you can answer the following questions in ASL.

1. What is the signer's name?

   Donnette Patterson

   _____

2. Where is she from?

   Colorado

   _____

3. What is her profession?

   She teaches at a community college

   _____

4. Who in her family is deaf?

    One set of grandparents is deaf. The other set is blind.

Study Questions

1. Replace this sign with another sign or signs that preserve the meaning as closely as possible.

    01:30:01;21

    Grandmother and grandfather

2. Replace this sign with another sign or signs that preserve the meaning as closely as possible.

    01:30:10;07

    Remember from a long time ago.

3. Replace this sign with another sign or signs that preserve the meaning as closely as possible.

01:30:10;28

Know what it is?

Want to know?

4. Replace this sign with another sign or signs that preserve the meaning as closely as possible.

01:30:23;10

How did we play it?

5. Replace this sign with another sign or signs that preserve the meaning as closely as possible.

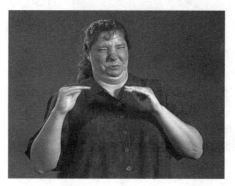

01:30:29;11

Young

6. Replace this sign with another sign or signs that preserve the meaning as closely as possible.

01:30:35;13

Ran very fast

7. Replace this sign with another sign or signs that preserve the meaning as closely as possible.

01:30:40;06

Used cane to find out where we were

8. Replace this sign with another sign or signs that preserve the meaning as closely as possible.

01:30:42;00

Ran all over the place

9. Replace this sign with another sign or signs that preserve the meaning as closely as possible.

01:30:43;11

Skilled

Good at

10. Replace this sign with another sign or signs that preserve the meaning as closely as possible.

01:31:00;24

I understand

Right

11. Replace this sign with another sign or signs that preserve the meaning as closely as possible.

01:31:01;25

Felt a bit silly

12. Replace this sign with other another sign or signs that preserve the meaning as closely as possible.

01:31:04;06

Valuable

Important

Touching

13. Replace this sign with another sign or signs that preserve the meaning as closely as possible.

01:31:05;21

Dead

Passed away

14. Replace this sign with another sign or signs that preserves the meaning as closely as possible.

01:31:08;13

Fade

Disappear

EXERCISE 3.3

At the Airport

DONNETTE PATTERSON

Directions

Student Workbook
page 71

Find this selection on the DVD. Watch the entire selection. Make sure you fully understand the entire selection before answering the study questions. Watch it again, if necessary. Answer each study question in the following manner. Record the original sign (indicated for you in the video captures) as exactly as possible. Watch the signer carefully. Record the sign or signs you will use to replace the original sign. Lexical substitution exercises increase your linguistic flexibility and mirroring the signing of a native signer increases your fluency.

Study Questions

1. Replace this sign with another sign or signs that preserve the meaning as closely as possible.

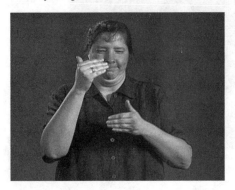

01:31:20;25

Procedure (fs)

Step by step process

2. Replace this sign with another sign or signs that preserve the meaning as closely as possible.

01:31:29;03

Explain

Tell

3. Replace this sign with other signs that preserve the meaning as closely as possible.

01:31:37;03

Remember

Make sure

Check

4. Replace this sign with another sign or signs that preserve the meaning as closely as possible.

01:31:39;13 to 01:31:41;10

Long-term parking

5. Replace this sign with another sign or signs that preserve the meaning as closely as possible.

01:31:46;19

Escalator (fs)

6. Replace this sign with another sign or signs that preserve the meaning as closely as possible.

01:31:51;05

Ticket counter (fs)

7. Replace this sign with another sign or signs that preserve the meaning as closely as possible.

01:31:53;08

People standing behind the counter

8. Replace this sign with another sign or signs that preserve the meaning as closely as possible

01:31:54;23

Usually

Most of the time

Typically

9. Replace this sign with another sign or signs that preserve the meaning as closely as possible.

01:31:55;23

Not friendly

Grumpy

10. Replace these signs with another sign or signs that preserve the meaning as closely as possible.

01:31:59;12

Stay calm

Relax

11. Replace this sign with another sign or signs that preserve the meaning as closely as possible.

01:32:03;17

Converse

Talk

12. Replace this sign with another sign or signs that preserve the meaning as closely as possible.

01:32:21;08

Very suspicious

13. Replace this sign with another sign or signs that preserve the meaning as closely as possible.

01:32:29;23 to **01:32:34;00**

X-ray machine

14. Replace this sign with another sign or signs that preserve the meaning as closely as possible.

01:32:35;28

Shoes off

15. Replace this sign with another sign or signs that preserve the meaning as closely as possible.

01:32:50;15

Walk along

16. Replace this sign with another sign or signs that preserve the meaning as closely as possible.

01:33:26;09

Really enjoy

Love

Progress Tracking Sheet

Use this sheet to track your progress with the exercises you have completed. After performing the exercise (one or two times) and answering the study questions, fill in the tracking sheet. Note the date that you completed the exercise and give an indication of your level of accomplishment. You can use either a quantitative or a qualitative approach to track your progress.

Exercise Number	Date	First Performance	Study Questions	Questions and Reminders	Date	Second Performance
Exercise 3.1 Quantitative						
Qualitative						
Exercise 3.2 Quantitative						
Qualitative						
Exercise 3.3 Quantitative						
Qualitative						
Quantitative Totals						

UNIT 4

Paraphrasing Propostitions

L arson (1984, p. 415) says, "Paraphrase is a restating of the same information in another way, sometimes with the addition of bits of information." Paraphrasing propositions means that you restate an entire idea unit using a different form. Paraphrasing in its strictest sense is an intralingual skill. Intralingual means within one language and does not involve two languages. People who are developing skills in a specific language often work to find various ways to say the same thing as a way of strengthening language skills. For example, a new signer of ASL may use an entire phrase to express a single sign if they do not know that sign. This new signer might something equivalent to "the machine which puts on paper the information from your computer screen" instead of the word "printer." Topics in this unit on paraphrasing propositions include the following.

Illocutionary force

Ambiguity

Unpacking propositions

Illocutionary Force

The illocutionary force of a message indicates whether it functions as a statement, command, or question. According to Larson (1984), illocutionary force is often conveyed by intonation in English. In other words, the tone of voice used by the signer will allow the listener to know whether the utterance "When are you going to take out the garbage?" is really a question or a statement regarding a chore that has not been done yet, but should have been done. The fact that this utterance is really a rhetorical question shows through the intonation pattern used when it is spoken. In ASL illocutionary force is indicated by non-manual grammar, including facial grammar and the intensity with which signs are expressed.

An indicator of a good interpretation is that it maintains the dynamics of the source language. The dynamics are conveyed thorough illocutionary force. This means that the receiver of the interpretation will receive the same impact in an interpreted message as the person who heard or saw the message in its original language. The interpreted message should have the same impact or emotional effect as the original. A successful interpretation is one that elicits the same response in those who are listening to the interpretation as it did in those who heard and understood the original. This is the ideal. However, in situations such as interpreting for a joke or other information that is very heavily culturally laden, it is very difficult to maintain the same level of illocutionary force in the target language.

Practice in preserving illocutionary force within a language is important because it allows you to determine whether the paraphrase has the same impact as the original. Preserving the illocutionary force means that even though the message is transferred from one language to another, the impact of the message in the source language should be roughly equivalent to the impact of the message in the target language.

Ambiguity

Ambiguity is the linguistic feature that can create uncertainty in the mind of the person receiving the message. This happens when the utterance has more than one possible meaning. Usually, the linguistic and social context where the utterance occurs can disambiguate the word or phrase, but not always. Even though we are focusing on intralingual skills now, when you begin interlingual exercise in translation or interpretation it is very important to clearly understand the source language before translating it. If a message is intentionally ambiguous in the source language, then the interpreter should strive to render a message in the target language that conveys approximately the same amount of ambiguity. For example, in some legal situations, the interrogator may intend to confuse the person being questioned and so uses ambiguous or unclear language. Ideally, the interpreter conveys the same amount of ambiguity. In reality, sometimes the utterance cannot be interpreted until the interpreter knows which meaning is intended.

Ambiguity can occur at the lexical level or at the phrase level. Words such as bed, pilot, free, plant, on, about, and many others in English have more than one meaning. The intended meaning is usually revealed by the context. In ASL pronouns can be ambiguous if you do not know what the referent is. For example, if the signer is pointing to a specific location in signing space and you do not know what or who the signer intends to refer to, you will sometimes be able to use context to clarify what is meant. Most interpreters have had the experience of realizing, after the fact, that they misunderstood a portion of the meaning of the message. The high stress levels that accompany most interpretation assignments often prevent interpreters from quickly realizing that the utterance was ambiguous and that more than one meaning is possible. When the stress of the situation has passed, and the assignment is completed, and the interpreter is no longer in the interpreting situation, the interpreter may suddenly realize, with a sinking feeling, that he or she conveyed the wrong message. This error could be due to not noticing the ambiguity and not dealing with it in real time by asking questions to clarify the meaning. Hopefully, the frequency of the occurrence of this kind of situation is reduced by practicing paraphrasing information in exercise format, removed from real interpretation situations. Later these skills can be applied in real-world situations in interpretation settings.

A certain amount of ability to tolerate ambiguity is required. Not all words or phrases that are ambiguous to the interpreter can be clarified. More mature students and interpreters may be able to tolerate greater amounts of ambiguity. Ambiguity can arise for a number of reasons. The signer may not really know what point he or she wishes to make. The signer may even intend to be ambiguous. Sometimes it will be difficult for the interpreter to follow the signer's line of reasoning and this can create uncertainty in the mind of the interpreter. The signer may not follow a prepared text. The signer may not show or tell the interpreter how the ideas being presented are related. In all of these situations the interpreter must convey the information as best they can. It may be necessary for the interpreter to stop the signer and ask for clarification.

Unpacking Propositions

When Larson (1984) uses the term "unpacking," she means that within each word it is possible to find more than one concept. The same is true of propositions or idea units. It is important for the interpreter to be able to quickly see as many relevant and possible ideas within each proposition as possible. This is a good beginning point for hypothesis testing. In other words, when an interpreter sees an ASL phrase, he or she should quickly try to grasp the various meanings that could be included in that phrase and then discard those hypotheses that are not relevant to the current linguistic and social context. For example, when the interpreter hears a phrase in English, "The mother is feeding her baby" as an exercise, the following propositions can be unpacked or delineated.

There is a woman.

There is a baby.

The woman may be the baby's mother.

The baby may be the child of the woman.

There is baby food.

The woman knows the baby is hungry.

The baby is hungry.

All of these are reasonable propositions that can be unpacked from the original sentence.

The following list of propositions could not be unpacked from the original because they assume too much information. These propositions may be true but their relevance cannot be determined from the original utterance.

The baby is a boy.

The baby is a girl.

The baby is allergic to eggs.

The mother likes feeding the baby.

The baby hates to be fed.

The baby wants the father to feed it.

The mother is late for work.

The practice of unpacking propositions reveals important ideas and can improve paraphrasing skills because this kind of exercise can help you see which ideas are really part of the concept and which are not. The accompanying exercises in ASL will allow you to develop skill in unpacking and better understanding the ASL concepts.

The Role of Paraphrasing

According to DeGroot (1997, p. 52),"Paraphrasing involves the conversion of a message expressed in given language into an equivalent message in the same language but worded differently." DeGroot goes on to point out that when paraphrasing between two spoken forms of the same language is done simultaneously, the demands of this task appear to be similar to those of simultaneous interpretation. "Not only do the two tasks share the requirement of simultaneous comprehension and production of speech, but unlike shadowing, they also both require a translation act, an act of recoding the same content in a different form." Other authors (Malakoff and Hakuta, 1991) suggest that intralingual paraphrasing is even more difficult than translation or interpretation because a larger vocabulary will be required to perform paraphrasing acts in a single language than is required to work across language boundaries.

Sometimes a single lexical item in the source language must be expressed in several words in the target language, such as when there is no single lexical equivalent in the target language. The converse of this can also be true. These situations call on paraphrasing skills to give the message the greatest impact. Paraphrasing is also used when idioms occur in the source language and do not have an equivalent expression in the target language. In that case the meaning of the idiom must be re-expressed in the target language in a way that is meaningful in that language.

Because there is generally not a one-to-one correspondence of lexical items across language boundaries, interpreters must have a variety of techniques they can use to accurately convey the meaning of the message from the source language into the target language. One of the most useful techniques in practice with conscious effort is the ability to quickly paraphrase a message within the source language and then to translate that paraphrased version of the message. In the process of simultaneous interpretation, it is possible that you might not realize that sometimes you paraphrase the source language before interpreting it. During the interpretation process, this paraphrase and subsequent interpretation of the paraphrase must be done with the highest possible speed and accuracy.

Paraphrasing Techniques

Occasionally during the interpretation process, an adequate interpretation does not appear in the mind of the interpreter. One good way to get out of such a "linguistic box" or problem is to paraphrase the original sentence and then interpret the paraphrased version. It is very important that the paraphrased version maintain the meaning of the original. For example, "There is a woman getting ready to go out the door" could be paraphrased as "A lady is prepared to leave via the exit." This paraphrase may seem a bit awkward, but it does not distort the meaning.

One paraphrasing technique is to substitute one sign at a time in the original sentence by finding synonyms. Again, this may lead to an awkward paraphrase, but that may not be a problem if the paraphrase maintains the meaning of the original utterance and provides you with a good point for beginning the interpretation. A word of caution: This does not mean that you should translate each sign in a sentence in order to arrive at the interpretation. Since most languages do not have corresponding lexical items, a sign-for-sign translation can rarely preserve the meaning of the original utterance.

A second possibility is reversing the clauses within the sentence. This can only be used if it does not change the meaning. For example, "Fred got sick from a tick bite in July and later in the summer he went to the doctor" can be paraphrased as "Fred went to the doctor last summer when he got sick after he was bitten by a tick." In the sentence, "John got up early, had breakfast and then went out to do his errands" cannot be paraphrased as "John did his errands, had breakfast and got up early." The meaning is not preserved in the second paraphrase. When the order of events is important to the meaning, then the order of events must appear in the same order in the paraphrase.

A third technique is to paraphrase the utterance into a more general form than the original sentence and still not skew the meaning. You can review the section on specific and general words to reinforce this topic. If the paraphrase is more specific, then the original meaning may be skewed. For example, "A baker is getting his bowls, rolling pin, pans and measuring cups out" can be paraphrased as "A baker is getting his baking utensils ready to use." The word "utensils" is a more general word and can include the items mentioned in the original sentence. If the sentence is "The baker is pouring batter into a pan," it cannot be paraphrased as "The man is putting batter into a springform pan." A springform pan is a specific type of pan and it is not implied by the original sentence. An acceptable paraphrase is "A man who knows how to bake is putting batter into a container."

These basic ways to approach paraphrasing, sign-for-sign substitution, changing the order of the propositions, and moving from specific to more general terms are all ways that you can improve your linguistic flexibility. Increased linguistic flexibility helps to form a strong foundation for accurate simultaneous interpretation skills as well as excellent self-expression skills.

Discussion Questions

Discuss the following questions with your students to promote insight and increase awareness of the importance of paraphrasing proposition skills as they relate to the interpretation process.

1. *How does an understanding of paraphrasing propositions in ASL relate to the interpretation process?*

    Practice in paraphrasing propositions can increase the range of grammatical constructions that are quickly available for the interpreter to use. When paraphrasing, it is important to preserve the meaning of the original message. Since the simultaneous interpretation process is so cognitively demanding, it is important to reduce cognitive effort wherever possible. One way to help reduce the effort needed is to practice specific components within the interpretation process. Be sure to point out to your students that it is necessary to practice paraphrasing within each of the languages that will be used in the interpretation process. Practice in this skill can provide great linguistic flexibility for the interpreter. It is quite common for students to find themselves repeating instead of paraphrasing. It will be important for you as the teacher to help students clearly see the difference between repetition and paraphrasing.

2. *How would you describe your ability to paraphrase propositions?*

    Ask this question before and after the practice exercises and see whether students feel that their skills improve and whether they have greater confidence in these skills. One difference that should become apparent is the difference between repetition and paraphrasing. Most students improve with increased focus and practice. Confidence in being able to find ways to restate ideas quickly is a benefit to the interpreter. Rapid and reliable propositional paraphrasing skills are not automatic, but rather must be learned and practiced. Asking this question before and after the exercises highlights the difference between having the impression of having the skill and actually having the skill.

3. *What will happen if the interpreter does not have rapid, reliable propositional paraphrasing skills?*

   When the interpreter does not have quick access to various ways to express the same concept, interpreter is limited in linguistic flexibility. When linguistic flexibility is limited, the richness of the product of the interpretation is compromised. For example, if an interpreter is working from English to ASL and only knows one way to interpret a phrase, the interpreter's work into ASL is limited in scope.

4. *What are some acceptable methods for paraphrasing? Here are a few methods that can be used in paraphrasing.*

   a. Replace lexical items with synonyms.

   b. Change the order of phrases.

   c. Use more general or more specific terms.

EXERCISES IN PARAPHRASING PROPOSITIONS

EXERCISE 4.1

Peeling Potatoes
ANNE MARIE BAER

Directions

Student Workbook
page 84

Find this selection on the DVD. Watch the first clip as many times as necessary to fully comprehend it and answer the questions in ASL. Space is provided for written answers. Watch the entire second clip. The selection is approximately one minute long. Review the selection as many times as necessary to fully understand it. Paraphrase the selection one sentence at a time and then provide a paraphrase for the title. Record your work. Answer the study questions.

Give an example of repeating compared to paraphrasing to demonstrate the difference between repetition and paraphrasing. The overall length of the paraphrase should be roughly equivalent to the original. If it is much shorter than the original it may be a summary instead of a paraphrase. If the paraphrase is much longer than the original, it may be more like elaborating on a topic than a paraphrase. Some answers are provided as a guide for you. Other answers may be acceptable.

The student paraphrases should not be direct repetitions of the original text.

Get to Know the Signer

This short segment allows you to get acquainted with the signer. Watch the selection and replay it until you can answer the following questions in ASL.

1. Where was she born and raised?

    Washington, DC

    _____

2. Where did her father grow up?

    Washington, DC

    _____

3. Where did her father go to school?

    Kendall School

    _____

4. What year did her father graduate from Gallaudet?

    1937

    _____

5. Where did her parents meet?

    Italy

    _____

6. Where was her mother from?

    Germany

    _____

7. When were they married?

    1957

    _____

8. How many children did her parents have?

   Four

   _____

9. Where did Anne Marie graduate from high school?

   California School for the Deaf in Fremont

   _____

10. What is Anne Marie currently studying?

    She is studying for an MA in linguistics.

    _____

11. What is her current job?

    She is an ASL rater and coordinator of the ASL/English mentoring program.

    _____

Study Questions

1. Do the original and your paraphrases convey approximately the same meaning? If you are not sure, ask for assistance or study the passages again and experiment with other possible solutions. Redo your paraphrases to better preserve the meaning of the original message.

2. Check each of your paraphrases to see whether the illocutionary force of each remains the same. If not, identify the paraphrase that caused a change in the illocutionary force by noting its timecode. Write the timecodes in the space provided.

   _____

3. Review your responses and check all of them, for ambiguity. If you find any instances of ambiguity, paraphrase again so that ambiguity is reduced. Record your new response.

   In some cases the original may be ambiguous. In such cases the paraphrase cannot be less ambiguous than the original. Conversely, in no case should the paraphrase be more ambiguous than the original.

EXERCISE 4.2

Feeding the Baby

ANNE MARIE BAER

Directions

Student Workbook
page 86

Find this video selection on your DVD and watch the entire selection. The video selection is approximately one minute long. Review the selection as many times as necessary to fully understand it. Paraphrase the selection one sentence at a time and then provide a paraphrase for the title. Record your work. Answer the study questions.

Study Questions

1. Review your paraphrases. Do your paraphrases preserve the meaning? If not, make a new recording that better preserves the meaning.

2. Check each of your paraphrases to see whether the illocutionary force of the original message is preserved. If not, determine where the illocutionary force is not preserved and make a new recording that better preserves the illocutionary force.

3. Check all of your responses for ambiguity. If you find any instances of ambiguity, paraphrase again so that ambiguity is reduced. Record your new response.

EXERCISE 4.3

Breaking Eggs

ANNE MARIE BAER

Directions

Student Workbook
page 87

Find this video selection on your DVD and watch the entire selection. The video selection is approximately one minute long. Review the selection as many times as necessary to fully understand it. Paraphrase the selection one sentence at a time and then provide a paraphrase for the title. Record your work. Answer the study questions.

Study Questions

1. Do the original and your paraphrases convey approximately the same meaning? If you are not sure, ask for assistance or study the passages again and experiment with other possible solutions. Redo your paraphrases to better preserve the meaning of the original message.

2. Check each of your paraphrases to see whether the illocutionary force of each remains the same. If not, identify the paraphrase that caused a change in the illocutionary force by noting its timecode in the space provided. Write the timecodes in the space provided.

   _____

3. Review your responses and check all of them for ambiguity. If you find any instances of ambiguity, paraphrase again so that ambiguity is reduced. Record your new response.

   In some cases the original may be ambiguous. In such cases the paraphrase cannot be less ambiguous than the original. Conversely, in no case should the paraphrase be more ambiguous than the original.

EXERCISE. 4.4

Culture Shock

MISSY KEAST

Directions

Student Workbook page 88

Find this selection on the DVD. Watch the first clip as many times as necessary to fully comprehend it. Space is provided for written answers. Watch the entire second clip. The selection is approximately 4 minutes long. Review the selection as many times as necessary to fully understand it. Paraphrase the selection one sentence at a time and then provide a paraphrase for the title. Record your work. Answer the study questions.

Get to Know the Signer

This short segment allows you to get acquainted with the signer. Watch the selection and replay it until you can answer the following questions in ASL.

1. Why does she prefer her older name sign?

    This was her name sign at the school for the deaf.

    _____

2. How many siblings does she have? How many are deaf? How many people in her family sign?

    Four. One. All of them.

    _____

3. How old is her daughter?

    Twenty months

    _____

4. How old will her grandmother be on her next birthday?

    100

    _____

5. What number granddaughter is Missy?

    68

    _____

6. Missy's daughter is what number great grandchild?

    62

    _____

7. How many immediate family members will be at the birthday party for her grandmother?

    300

    _____

Study Questions

1. Do the original and your paraphrases convey the same meaning? If you are not sure, ask for assistance or study the passages again and experiment with other possible solutions. Redo your paraphrases to better preserve the meaning of the original message.

2. Check each of your paraphrases to see whether the illocutionary force of each remains the same. If not, identify the paraphrase that caused a change in the illocutionary force by noting its timecode in the space provided. Record a revised paraphrase.

   _____

3. Review your responses and check all of them for ambiguity. If you find any instances of ambiguity, paraphrase again so that ambiguity is reduced. Record your new response.

Progress Tracking Sheet

Use this sheet to track your progress with the exercises you have completed. After performing the exercise (one or two times) and answering the study questions, fill in the tracking sheet. Note the date that you completed the exercise and give an indication of your level of accomplishment. You can use either a quantitative or a qualitative approach to track your progress.

Exercise Number	Date	First Performance	Study Questions	Questions and Reminders	Date	Second Performance
Exercise 4.1 Quantitative						
Qualitative						
Exercise 4.2 Quantitative						
Qualitative						
Exercise 4.3 Quantitative						
Qualitative						
Exercise 4.4 Quantitative						
Qualitative						
Quantitative Totals						

UNIT

5 *Paraphrasing Discourse*

Paraphrasing at the discourse level is retelling a story or text in different signs than the original. Review the information in Unit 4 on paraphrasing propositions. All of the constraints of paraphrasing information at the sentence level apply to paraphrasing at the discourse level. A paraphrase of discourse level text should contain the same information as the original, but is not an exact repetition.

In general, when practicing paraphrasing, it is advisable to keep the information in the paraphrase in the same order as the information in the original. If the interpreter believes that the order of events is inconsequential, that may change the cause-and-effect relationship between events in the text. Keeping the events in the same order and relationship to each other is one way to reduce errors in interpretation. Giving directions or instructions is an example where the order of information must be preserved exactly. In other kinds of texts, the exact order of information can be less crucial. In cases where the order of information is less crucial, the paraphrase need not necessarily preserve the order of information. Sometimes phrases can be rearranged as long as the message is preserved.

In paraphrasing it is very important to preserve the meaning of the original as much as possible, keeping in mind that a change in form changes the meaning slightly. The original message and the paraphrased message should convey meanings that are as similar as possible. When you practice paraphrasing with this intent, you lay a strong foundation for achieving a faithful interpretation because paraphrasing practice makes you acutely aware of specific meanings within languages. This increased sensitivity to meaning within languages will eventually enhance interpretation skills.

Length of Paraphrase

A paraphrased text should convey the meaning of the original text. Some features should also be held constant. For example, if the original had an introduction and conclusion, then so should the paraphrase. It is very important to remember that the overall length of the original message and the paraphrased message could be different. For example, in ASL a sign commonly glossed as BORED could *require* several signs to paraphrase it, so the paraphrase will be longer than the original message. This is unpacking and although the paraphrase is longer in form it is not actually an expansion; it is merely a paraphrase. The form of the original and the paraphrase will be different, but the meaning should remain as constant as possible.

ASL: ME BORED HOMEWORK

ASL paraphrase: ME DON'T WANT fs-DO HOMEWORK

Likewise, several lexical items in ASL can result in a paraphrase that is a single sign. Notice that the form is different but that the message is conveyed and that length is not the main criterion for determining success. Either form would be linguistically appropriate in ASL.

ASL: CAUGHT-ME, WISH NOT

ASL Paraphrase: GULP (closing fist on throat)

Even though we are focusing only on intralingual skills in this volume, it is important to note that we are working on these skills as a foundation for interlingual skills that follow such as translation and consecutive and simultaneous interpreting. These concepts regarding length of utterance also apply to interlingual acts such as translation and interpretation. There is not a one-to-one correspondence between ASL and English words. We expect that sometimes the source language will express an idea in a single word and the target language will require several signs to convey the meaning. It is possible that an ASL sign will require several English words in order to convey approximately the same message. Note that this is not really "expanding" the message in English; rather, this is the linguistically appropriate way to render the message.

Also, when interpreting from ASL to English (note that the commonly used term 'voicing' actually is a misnomer since 'voice' is not a language), since there is not a one-to-one correspondence of lexical items, there may be an ASL phrase that contains several signs that can be conveyed in English using fewer English words. This does not imply that ASL must be "compressed" or "reduced" before translating it into English. Assuming or implying that one language must be compressed, reduced, or, conversely, expanded in order to make an interlingual transfer assumes an underlying symmetry between two languages which would then make it possible to add or subtract from one to create an equivalent in the other (see Snell-Hornby, 1995, pp. 1–30 for additional information).

ASL gloss: CHERISH

English equivalent: I adore you.

When interpreting from English to ASL it is possible that the source message in English will contain several words while the ASL interpretation will require only a single sign. This is not really compressing or reducing the message. Interpretation requires that the interpreter be aware of the most appropriate way to express the message in the target language regardless of its length.

English source message: I adore you

ASL interpretation: CHERISH

English source message: You are so skilled

ASL interpretation: F – on chin

Since ASL and English have different grammatical structures it is clear that comparing two languages on the same scale in terms of length of utterance is likely to provide a faulty foundation for mastering the interpretation process. When you are working between English and ASL it is not necessary to amplify concepts in order to make the message linguistically appropriate. Rather, it is necessary to be linguistically sophisticated enough to know how to achieve a faithful rendition of a message into the target language without focusing on the number of signs or words in the utterances. In order to develop the type of linguistic sophistication necessary to make interlingual transfers, it is crucial to study various ways of expressing a message within a language while minimizing distortion of the message.

Two things determine the actual form of the paraphrase. The first is comprehending the source text. The second major factor is expressive ability in the language. The greater the range of expressive language, the better the paraphrasing process will become. Aptitudes in comprehension and expression contribute to ease in paraphrasing.

Question Forms and Functions

Quick and accurate identification of the various forms and functions of language is essential to rapid and accurate paraphrasing. Statements generally convey information. Commands order someone to do something. A more complicated situation arises in relation to question forms. Kearsely (1976) provides a good summary on questions and their forms and functions. He says that gestures that accompany a question, as well as the syntax, can help identify question forms and functions. Some questions seek to gain information, such as "What would you like for lunch?" Other questions serve to provide information. The question "Are you ready to order?" conveys the fact that the waiter is ready to take your order. Rhetorical questions generally function as statements of information or clarification rather than attempts to gain information. Sometimes questions serve to draw attention to a point. For example, in a lecture setting, the teacher may ask, "Is everyone ready to take the quiz?" Occasionally, questions are repeated by the listener back to the questioner. When this happens, the purpose is usually to buy some time rather than provide information to the questioner. This is called "echoic" questioning.

Question *forms* include the following types of questions.

1. *Yes/No questions.* These require a "yes" or "no" response. In ASL these questions are marked by raised eyebrows.

2. *Why questions.* These seek information and in English begin with a "wh" word such as what, who, why, where, or when. In ASL these question forms are indicated by a furrowed brow.

Question *functions* include the following.

1. *Closed questions.* Some questions seek information that can be answered with yes or no. For example, "Can I borrow your bus schedule?" This question can be answered with only a limited number of responses. The usual answers will be "yes," "no" or "maybe." Another possible answer is "I'm using it now." This answer functions as a "no."

2. *Open-ended Questions.* Some questions require more of an answer than just yes or no. An example of an open-ended question is "How do you feel about buying a used car?" The answer can include a wide variety of information, but not a yes or no answer.

The Role of Paraphrasing at the Discourse Level

Rendering the same message in a different form is a valuable way to develop skills in determining how well you are preserving the message within a language. When you become sensitized to the nuances in meaning *within* a language you are better able to determine when the paraphrased version conveys the meaning and intent of the original. This type of practice develops a sophistication that will provide a strong foundation for developing skills in determining fidelity in interlingual exercises. Effective translation, consecutive interpreting, and simultaneous interpreting are all contingent upon accurate decisions about message preservation.

Even though interpreters are obliged to remain faithful to the message, the link between ability in maintaining intralingual fidelity and interlingual fidelity may have been weak or not explicitly shown in the literature. It is imperative to have a firm command of the notion that there is not a one-to-one correspondence between lexical items in ASL and English. One way to help promote this understanding is to practice within ASL and realize that when a sign is paraphrased, it may require several signs instead of one. That is so because languages are not isomorphic, there is always not a one-to-one correspondence between words in various languages. If this is true within a language, it is also true across language boundaries.

If you develop a strong sense of how to preserve a message within a language, then judgments about interlingual message preservation will be within your grasp. Most importantly, you will be able to determine when the target language rendition in simultaneous interpretation is skewed and will be able to make repairs to the message to make it equivalent. Deliberate practice in paraphrasing creates a sense of confidence about making decisions about fidelity. It is best to practice paraphrasing in your first language first and then in your second language.

Intralingual paraphrasing requires creating as near to equivalent messages as possible with two forms in the same language. Since the process of simultaneous interpretation is far more cognitively demanding than paraphrasing, spending time developing accurate paraphrasing skills will reduce the cognitive load when further skills in the interpretation process are developed.

Discussion Questions

Discuss the following questions with your students to promote insight and increase awareness of the importance of the ability to paraphrasing discourse, particularly as this skill relates to the interpretation process.

1. *How does an understanding of paraphrasing in ASL relate to the interpretation process?*

    Being able to quickly rearrange propositions without changing the meaning is an important skill in interpretation because this skill allows for greater flexibility in finding a good starting point for the translation process. Most importantly, paraphrasing helps to build a strong foundation for maintaining fidelity within and eventually between languages.

Be sure to point out that it is necessary to practice this skill within each of the languages that will be used in the interpretation process. Practicing the skill of paraphrasing discourse can provide great linguistic flexibility for the interpreter regardless of language pair.

2. *Do you feel you have strong discourse paraphrasing skills?*

Ask this question before and after the drills and see whether skills have improved and whether students have greater confidence in their skill. Most students improve with increased focus and practice. Rapid and reliable paraphrasing skills are not automatic, but rather must be learned and practiced. Emphasize the importance of developing equivalence between the original and paraphrased versions of messages.

3. *What happens if the interpreter does not have rapid, reliable discourse paraphrasing skills?*

The interpreter who does not have rapid and reliable discourse paraphrasing skills will find it more difficult to find the gist of the speech. Finding the gist of the speech allows the interpreter to be able to organize the ideas as they are presented. Second, the ability to paraphrase may lead to a more reliable interpretation of the message because this skill relies on being able to determine equivalence.

4. *What are some acceptable methods for paraphrasing discourse?*

Here are a few methods that can be used in paraphrasing discourse. Some of these methods are the same as those used for paraphrasing at the proposition level.

a. Replace lexical items with synonyms.

b. Change the order of phrases. This can only be used in discourse level paraphrase if the change in the order does not change the overall meaning of the passage or paragraph. Remember that a paraphrase is not a repetition nor a summary.

5. *If a paraphrased message results in a longer version, is that really expanding the message or paraphrasing the message?*

It is important for students to have a firm command of the notion that there is not a one-to-one correspondence between lexical items in ASL and English. One way to help promote this understanding is to practice within ASL and demonstrate that when a sign is paraphrased, it may require several signs instead of one. If this is true within a language, it is also true across language boundaries because languages are not isomorphic.

EXERCISES IN PARAPHRASING DISCOURSE

Decide whether you want to conduct this exercise in class or whether you want the students to do this exercise on their own time.

Read the directions and explain them to the students. Allow time for questions after you give the directions. You should plan on at least 5 minutes to prepare the students for the exercise. Five minutes should be enough if you have the group's attention and if all equipment is ready and in working order.

EXERCISE 5.1

Memorable Experience
BROOKE BUDZINSKI

Directions

Student Workbook page 96

Find this exercise on the DVD. This first segment allows you to get acquainted with the signer. You do not need to record your responses. You may write your answer in the space provided. Watch the second clip. The selection is about 2 minutes long. Watch once and paraphrase the entire selection to the best of your ability. Review the selection as many times as needed in order to fully comprehend it. Record a second paraphrase of the passage. You may do the paraphrase in segments if necessary but the segments should be longer than a single phrase. Answer the rest of the study questions.

The passage is 2 minutes long. You can use this passage for a warm-up. Go over the passage with your students in a group to be sure that everyone has fully understood the passage. If 2 minutes is too long, you can ask the students to paraphrase shorter segments.

Get to Know the Signer

This short segment allows you to get acquainted with the signer. Watch the selection and replay it until you can answer the following questions in ASL.

1. Where did she grow up?

   Wisconsin

2. When did she enter Gallaudet University?

    Fall 1998

    _____

3. What happened after she graduated?

    Her parents divorced and her mother moved to Virginia. Brooke also moved to Virginia.

    _____

4. What does Brooke do now?

    She teaches ASL at a community college.

    _____

Study Questions

1. Watch your first and second paraphrases and compare them to the video-text. Which paraphrase is more accurate? Why? Record your answers on your videotape. You may write your answer in the space provided.

    _____

    _____

2. Does your second paraphrase convey approximately the same meaning as the original? If you are not sure whether your paraphrase preserves the meaning, compare each idea unit in the original with each idea unit in your response. If your paraphrase does not convey the same meaning, examine it to determine why.

    _____

    _____

3. Is the information in the same order? Would changing the order change the meaning? Find one example of where your paraphrase is longer than the original. Find one example of where your paraphrase is shorter than the original. Is the message preserved regardless of the length?

Example: Can be paraphrased as NEVER FORGET.

4. Did you include all of the information that was presented in the original? If ideas were omitted, note them here and record yourself providing a more complete version.

5. Check for question forms in the source and in your paraphrases. Are there any instances where your paraphrase would have been enhanced by using a question form? Record your improved version.

EXERCISE 5.2

Hearing People Are Normal After All
MINNE MAE WILDING DIAZ

Directions

Student Workbook
page 98

Find this exercise on the DVD. This first segment allows you to get acquainted with the signer. You do not need to record your responses. You may write your answer in the space provided. Watch the second clip. The selection is about 3 minutes long. Watch once and paraphrase the entire selection to the best of your ability. Review the selection as many times as needed in order to fully comprehend it. Record a second paraphrase of the passage. You may do the paraphrase in segments if necessary but the segments should be longer than a single phrase. Answer the rest of the study questions.

Get to Know the Signer

This short segment allows you to get acquainted with the signer. Watch the selection and replay it until you can answer the following questions in ASL.

1. Is her family hearing or deaf?

    Deaf

    _____

2. Where did she grow up?

    Idaho

    _____

3. Are her husband and children hearing or deaf?

    They are all deaf.

    _____

Study Questions

1. Watch your first and second paraphrases and compare them to the video-text. Which paraphrase is more accurate? Why? Record your answers in the space provided and also on your videotape.

    _____

    _____

2. Does your second paraphrase convey approximately the same meaning as the original? If you are not sure whether your paraphrase preserves the meaning, compare each idea unit in the original with each idea unit in your response. If your paraphrase does not convey the same meaning, examine it to determine why. Record your improved version.

    _____

    _____

3. Is the information in the same order? Would changing the order change the meaning?

    _____

    _____

4. Find one example of where your paraphrase is longer than the original. Find one example of where your paraphrase is shorter than the original. Is the message preserved regardless of the length?

_____

_____

5. Did you include all of the information that was presented in the original? If ideas were omitted, note them here and record yourself providing a more complete version.

_____

6. Check for question forms in the source and in your paraphrases. Are there any instances where your paraphrase would have been enhanced by using a question form?

_____

EXERCISE 5.3

My Work in the Auto Body Shop
UZI BUZGALO

Directions

Student Workbook
page 100

Find this exercise on the DVD. This first segment allows you to get acquainted with the signer. Watch the selection and replay it until you can answer the following questions in ASL. You do not need to record your responses. You may write your answer in the space provided. Watch the second clip. The selection is about 4 minutes long. Watch once and paraphrase the entire selection to the best of your ability. Review the selection as many times as needed in order to fully comprehend it. Record a second paraphrase of the passage. You may do the paraphrase in segments if necessary but the segments should be longer than a single phrase. Answer the rest of the study questions.

Get to Know the Signer

This short segment allows you to get acquainted with the signer. Watch the selection and replay it until you can answer the following questions in ASL.

1. Where was he born?

    Afula, Israel

    _____

2. Was it a metropolitan area or a rural area?

    It was rural.

    _____

3. Was it a monolingual area?

    No, many different languages were used there.

    _____

4. How did he communicate with his parents?

    Through writing and drawing.

    _____

5. Where did he move to when he was 5?

    Jerusalem

    _____

6. How many students were at the school for the deaf in Jerusalem?

    40

    _____

7. Where did he attend high school?

    Tel Aviv

    _____

8. What did he study?

   He learned to become a mechanic.

_____

Study Questions

1. Watch your first and second paraphrases and compare them to the video-text. Which paraphrase is more accurate? Why? Record your answers in the space provided and in ASL on your videotape.

_____

_____

2. Does your second paraphrase convey approximately the same meaning as the original? If you are not sure whether your paraphrase preserves the meaning, compare each idea unit in the original with each idea unit in your response. If your paraphrase does not convey the same meaning, examine it to determine why. Record an improved version.

_____

_____

3. Is the information in the same order? Would changing the order change the meaning?

_____

_____

4. Find one example of where your paraphrase is longer than the original. Find one example of where your paraphrase is shorter than the original. Is the message preserved regardless of the length?

_____

_____

5. Did you include all of the information that was presented in the original? If ideas were omitted, note them here and record yourself providing a more complete version.

    _____

6. Check for question forms in the source and in your paraphrases. Are there any instances where your paraphrase would have been enhanced by using a question form?

    _____

    _____

Progress Tracking Sheet

Use this sheet to track your progress with the exercises you have completed. After performing the exercise (one or two times) and answering the study questions, fill in the tracking sheet. Note the date that you completed the exercise and give an indication of your level of accomplishment. You can use either a quantitative or a qualitative approach to track your progress.

Exercise Number	Date	First Performance	Study Questions	Questions and Reminders	Date	Second Performance
Exercise 5.1 Quantitative						
Qualitative						
Exercise 5.2 Quantitative						
Qualitative						
Exercise 5.3 Quantitative						
Qualitative						
Quantitative Totals						

UNIT

6

Visual Form and Meaning

*T*he goal of this unit is to improve awareness of the difference between form and meaning and how this difference is crucial in the interpretation process. Read the introductory information in this unit. If you have other information you want to present to your students on the topic of visual form and meaning, prepare that information in an outline to refer to during your lecture. Ask students to discuss the terms "visual form" and "meaning" and see what they believe these terms mean. Discussion questions are included and should precede the exercises.

In this unit, the goal is to emphasize the difference between meaning as conveyed in a graphic (picture) representation and the same idea or meaning expressed in ASL. This unit further deepens the understanding that the form of a message can vary while the meaning can remain constant. There are two representations of form found in the exercises in this unit. The forms are the visual image (picture) and the ASL created in response to the visual image. The exercises will give you practice in expressing ideas in ASL and comparing your work with that of a fluent signer. These exercises develop a greater awareness of the importance of remaining faithful to the original message, which provides a strong foundation for translation and interpretation.

Working from a visual image to a signed form is a particularly effective way to improve intralingual skills because the visual images present concepts and the relationships between objects in the pictures in a manner that is not reliant upon written or spoken English or ASL. Kintsch (1972) explains that concepts can contain meaning and information about relationships that do not rely on a specific language. The visual images in the study set will prompt you to express the signs that correspond to the objects shown in the pictures and the relationships between them without being influenced by spoken, written, or signed forms that convey the same idea.

According to Larsen (1984, p. 3) the form of a language consists of its words, phrases, clauses, and sentences that are spoken or written. These forms are also referred to as the surface structure of a language. The meaning is the sense or semantics or deep structure of the message. The issue of form and meaning is central to the study of interpretation, regardless of the languages involved. It is crucial that interpreters know the difference between form and meaning and how this difference can affect the interpretation.

Topics in this unit include the following.

Faithful translation

Form

Meaning

Visual image

Faithful Translation

According to Nida and Tabor (1984), a faithful translation evokes essentially the same response as the original message. "The receptor understands the same meaning and reacts emotionally in the same way and comes to the same decisions and actions as the original receptors. Faithfulness is primarily a quality of the message rather than the form and results from dynamic equivalence rather than formal correspondence" (p.201).

Fidelity guides us in determining what to include in our rendition. Practicing fidelity prepares us to deal with issues of remaining faithful to the message during interlingual transfers such as translation and interpretation.

As you do the exercises, think carefully about what is warranted by the picture or can be inferred from it. Sometimes this awareness can help you determine how much detail you should include in your ASL rendition. If you use several signs to express an idea, it is not really adding or expanding as long as the meaning is preserved and is consistent with the meaning shown in the picture. Keep in mind that you are building a foundation for fidelity in translation and interpretation. Likewise, since no two languages have the same form or rules of expression, the utterances generated in response to the pictures could be short. This does not mean that the message is truncated or compressed as long as the form is natural to ASL and the meaning is preserved.

Form

The form of the message is the observable part of the language. In ASL it is the signed version of the message and includes information at the word level (vocabulary), phrase, sentence, and discourse level. The form is the part of language that can be seen or heard.

Meaning

The meaning is the non-observable part of communication. The sense, intent, and message are "clothed" or expressed in a form. The meaning is the central kernel or idea that must be clearly understood and conveyed by the ASL rendition.

Visual Image

The visual images used in this book are simple line drawings that have meaning without written, signed, or spoken language. Relationships between persons or persons and objects are shown in these simple pictures. No two signers will respond in exactly the same way to these pictures. These differences in expression emphasize that a message can be conveyed in several forms without changing the meaning of the message. Each person has a different set of life and linguistic experiences and level of language competence. These differences in experience and language competence will affect the way people see and respond to the pictures.

The Role of Distinguishing Form from Meaning

Interpreters must be able to convey the meaning from the source language, the language they are working from, into the target language, the language they are working into, without distorting the message. If interpreters follow the form of the source language when they render the message in the target language, there is a high probability that the interpretation will not accurately convey the intended message. An example of this kind of problem can be seen when an interpreter follows the word order of the source language when interpreting into the target language, which has a different set of rules for word order. Here the terms "word" and "sign" are used interchangeably. When interpreters follow the form of the source language and disregard the meaning, the result can be a word-for-word transcoding process. The word-for-word approach rarely conveys the intended meaning accurately. Instead, the result is often "word salad." The words presented in the target language may look or seem acceptable in proximity to each other, just as the components in a salad do, but they have no real relationship to each other. The ideal situation in interpretation is one in which the interpreter has grasped the intended meaning. Then, regardless of the form of the source language, the message is rendered in a syntax and vocabulary that is appropriate to the target language. The better the interpreter understands the meaning, the better chance he or she will have in rendering the message into a form that is appropriate to the target language.

The issue of the difference between form and meaning is further complicated by the fact that often one word or form can have many meanings in a specific language. For example, the word "run" in English has many meanings but only one form. On the other hand, a single meaning or concept in the source language may have many different words to express it in the target language. For example, the ASL sign that is glossed as "SILLY" will require one or more English words to convey its meaning, depending on context.

Interpreters must be able to determine the intended meaning of the message in the source language and which form in the target language most appropriately expresses the intended meaning. This decision will ultimately be based on many factors. Some of these factors can include the context of the message, the participants, and the cultural aspects of the languages and situation as well as the interpreter's level of language ability in both the source and the target languages. These factors make it necessary to be able to make quick linguistic decisions during the interpretation process. Structured practice and experience can improve the interpreter's linguistic decision-making.

Discussion Questions

Discuss the following questions with your students to promote insight and increase awareness of the importance of understanding the difference between form and meaning expressed in ASL.

1. *How does an understanding of the difference between form and meaning relate to the interpretation process?*

    Most students have not had the opportunity to study ASL with regard to the differences between form and meaning. Interpreters must be aware that many different forms of ASL could represent a single visual image. This awareness can provide the interpreter great linguistic flexibility.

2. *Do you feel you understand a visual image the same way everyone else does?*

    Most students will answer "yes" to this question. This question does not seek to see whether the interpreter is an objective observer. Hopefully, the interpreter is objective. This question encourages the student to see that each person who views a simple picture may see it differently than anyone else. The belief that everyone sees things the same way leads users of the same language to believe that they are communicating clearly and understand each other well. In fact, even between two people conversing in the same language, there is usually some loss of intended meaning.

3. *What happens when two people see the same visual image differently?*

    First, the two viewers are not likely to realize that they do not see the same things in the visual image. If one or both viewers can realize that there are various ways to see an image, then there is less likelihood that misunderstandings will arise between the two people. If the misunderstanding occurs between friends, a conflict may arise. If the misunderstanding occurs between people who are not of equal status in the context of that conversation, usually the person of lower status will be disadvantaged by the misunderstanding. As students develop more awareness of how often people misunderstand each other, it is likely that they will be tempted to explain meanings and misunderstandings to people who are conversing in the same language. Should they? This could become an interesting discussion of the interpreter's role, which generally does not include clearing up misunderstandings between signers of the same language.

Naturally, each person will have a different "form" or way of expressing what he or she sees in the picture. Through these expressions of form, we can determine whether we see approximately the same things in a visual image or not.

4. *What will happen if the interpreter does not understand the message conveyed in the visual image but thinks they do understand?*

   This is a common situation. When the interpreter misunderstands, then the interpretation will be skewed or inaccurate, whether the interpreter is aware of the misunderstanding or not.

5. *What happens when the interpreter does not understand the message conveyed in the visual image and knows that they do not understand?*

   This lack of understanding should become apparent very quickly. The interpreter or student will not be able to give linguistic form to the visual image. The interpreter will not be able to proceed until he or she has understood the message.

EXERCISES IN VISUAL IMAGES WHOSE MEANING IS CONVEYED IN ASL

In this section, the goal is to emphasize the difference between form and meaning. Visual images are presented in the study set. In the accompanying DVD, a native user of ASL, Anne Marie Baer, shows her understandings of the pictures through ASL. Her instructions were to look at the entire set of pictures on the page and create a response or sentence that conveys the meaning of each picture on the page. You will create your own responses to the same visual images. As you compare your ASL to that of Anne Marie, it will become clear that the meaning of the pictures can and will be expressed in slightly different forms, depending on the way a person chooses to express themselves in ASL and their fluency in the language. Even though you and Anne Marie are looking at the same pictures, it is unlikely that any two sentences used to convey the meaning of a specific picture will be exactly the same. So even though the forms are different, the meaning can remain constant. It is also true that variations in expression (form) can slightly alter the meaning. Comparing meanings of the signers' sentences with your sentences will help you understand how differences in form can change the meaning of the sentence.

These short practice exercise scenarios do not contain contextual or cultural information. Additional context can be added for variety in these exercises. For example, you could say that this set of pictures depicts an event that occurred in the 1930s or that the people in the pictures are from a culture other than your own.

Please note that each sentence shown on the DVD represents the signers' view and manner of expression. When working from a picture to a signed form, you will notice that sometimes details can be left out or added. Sometimes, details are added that can't be determined from the pictures. You will consider whether omissions or additions are warranted by the pictures shown in the exercise, keeping in mind that fidelity is of the utmost importance.

In the following exercises, you will respond in ASL and record your responses. Later, you will compare your responses to those of Anne Marie Baer, the signer.

The exercises in this unit are designed to introduce the concepts related to distinguishing form from meaning. The first exercise is meant to be used as a warm-up and to be discussed in group format. You could conduct this exercise in class if students can record themselves during class time. Alternatively, students can do the work out of class. In either case, students must record their responses.

If you decide to do this exercise in class, each student must be able to record his or her answers on a video recorder. Read the directions and explain them to the students. Allow time for questions after you have given the directions. You should plan on at least 5 minutes to prepare the students for the exercise. Five minutes should be enough if you have the group's attention and if all equipment is ready and in working order.

EXERCISE 6.1

Gardening

ANNE MARIE BAER

Directions

Student Workbook
page 109

Look at the pictures and record your responses in ASL. Look at all nine pictures for Exercise 6.1. Record one complete sentence for each of the nine pictures. Your sentence should include only the information that is warranted by the picture and that expresses your understanding of the picture. You should not add or subtract information. Pause after each sentence and think about the information you wish to include in the next sentence. Watch Anne Marie's responses and answer the study questions.

Study Questions

1. Watch each of Anne Marie's nine sentences. Then watch each of your recorded sentences. For each sentence note in the space below whether the *form* is exactly the same or different between the two versions.

	Same	*Different*
Sentence 1		
Sentence 2		
Sentence 3		
Sentence 4		
Sentence 5		
Sentence 6		
Sentence 7		
Sentence 8		
Sentence 9		

2. Watch each of Anne Marie's nine sentences. Then watch each of your recorded sentences. For each sentence note in the space below whether the *meaning* is exactly the same or different between the two versions.

	Same	*Different*
Sentence 1		
Sentence 2		
Sentence 3		
Sentence 4		
Sentence 5		
Sentence 6		
Sentence 7		
Sentence 8		
Sentence 9		

3. Review your sentences to determine whether you have included any information that is not warranted by the picture. Note in the spaces below whether your rendition is faithful to the message. If not, explain what needs to be changed to make your rendition more faithful.

Faithful (Yes, No)   *Why*

Sentence 1 _____

Sentence 2 _____

Sentence 3 _____

Sentence 4 _____

Sentence 5 _____

Sentence 6 _____

Sentence 7 _____

Sentence 8 _____

Sentence 9 _____

4. Study Anne Marie's responses. Rerecord your sentences again, following features you observe in her work to achieve greater fluency and to improve your ASL syntax.

5. Review your second recording. Do your sentences preserve the meaning of the pictures without addition or omission?

_____

_____

Directions

Student Workbook page 112

EXERCISE 6.2

Going Fishing

ANNE MARIE BAER

Look at the pictures and record your responses in ASL. Look at all nine pictures for Exercise 6.2. Record one complete sentence for each of the nine pictures. Your sentence should include only the information that is warranted by the picture and that expresses your understanding of the picture. You should not add or subtract information. Pause after each sentence and think about the information you wish to include in the next sentence. Watch Anne Marie's responses and answer the study questions.

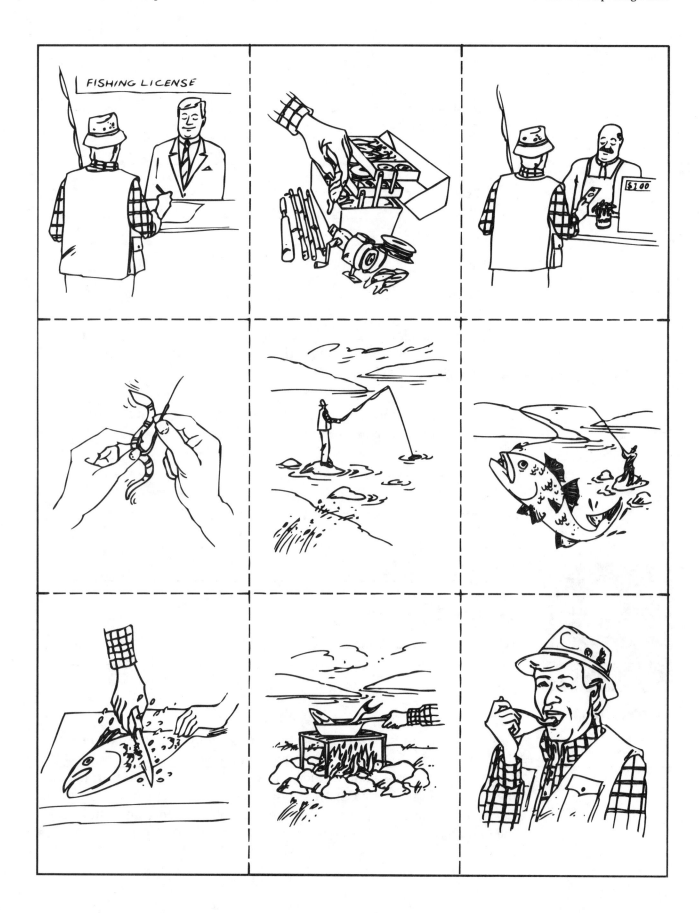

Study Questions

1. Watch each of Anne Marie's nine sentences. Then watch each of your recorded sentences. For each sentence note in the space below whether the *form* is exactly the same or different between the two versions.

	Same	*Different*
Sentence 1		
Sentence 2		
Sentence 3		
Sentence 4		
Sentence 5		
Sentence 6		
Sentence 7		
Sentence 8		
Sentence 9		

2. Watch each of Anne Marie's nine sentences. Then watch each of your recorded sentences. For each sentence note in the space below whether the *meaning* is exactly the same or different between the two versions.

	Same	*Different*
Sentence 1		
Sentence 2		
Sentence 3		
Sentence 4		
Sentence 5		
Sentence 6		
Sentence 7		
Sentence 8		
Sentence 9		

3. Review your sentences to determine whether you have included any information that is not warranted by the picture. Note in the spaces below whether your rendition is faithful to the message. If not, explain what needs to be changed to make your rendition more faithful.

	Faithful (Yes, No)	*Why*
Sentence 1		
Sentence 2		
Sentence 3		
Sentence 4		
Sentence 5		
Sentence 6		
Sentence 7		
Sentence 8		
Sentence 9		

4. Study Anne Marie's responses. Rerecord your sentences again, following features you observe in her work to achieve greater fluency and to improve your ASL syntax.

5. Review your second recording. Do your sentences preserve the meaning of the pictures without addition or omission?

_____

_____

EXERCISE 6.3

Building a Table

ANNE MARIE BAER

Directions

Student Workbook
page 115

Look at the pictures and record your responses in ASL. Look at all nine pictures for exercise 6.3. Record one complete sentence for each of the nine pictures. Your sentence should include only the information that is warranted by the picture and that expresses your understanding of the picture. You should not add or subtract information. Pause after each sentence and think about the information you wish to include in the next sentence. Watch Anne Marie's responses and answer the study questions.

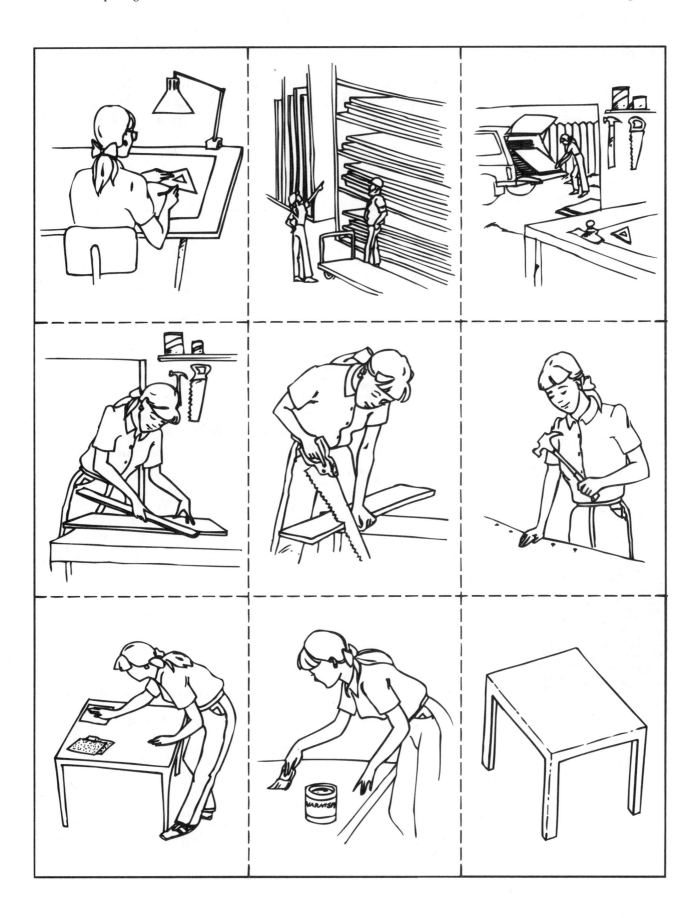

Study Questions

1. Watch each of Anne Marie's nine sentences. Then watch each of your recorded sentences. For each sentence note in the space below whether the *form* is exactly the same or different between the two versions.

	Same	*Different*
Sentence 1		
Sentence 2		
Sentence 3		
Sentence 4		
Sentence 5		
Sentence 6		
Sentence 7		
Sentence 8		
Sentence 9		

2. Watch each of Anne Marie's nine sentences. Then watch each of your recorded sentences. For each sentence note in the space below whether the *meaning* is exactly the same or different between the two versions.

	Same	*Different*
Sentence 1		
Sentence 2		
Sentence 3		
Sentence 4		
Sentence 5		
Sentence 6		
Sentence 7		
Sentence 8		
Sentence 9		

3. Review your sentences to determine whether you have included any information that is not warranted by the picture. Note in the spaces below whether your rendition is faithful to the message. If not, explain what needs to be changed to make your rendition more faithful.

	Faithful (Yes, No)	*Why*

Sentence 1 _____

Sentence 2 _____

Sentence 3 _____

Sentence 4 _____

Sentence 5 _____

Sentence 6 _____

Sentence 7 _____

Sentence 8 _____

Sentence 9 _____

4. Study Anne Marie's responses. Rerecord your sentences again, following features you observe in her work to achieve greater fluency and to improve your ASL syntax.

5. Review your second recording. Do your sentences preserve the meaning of the pictures without addition or omission?

_____

_____

Additional Exercises at the Sentence Level to Compare Form and Meaning

1. Use the sentences you created and change them to negative sentences. How does this change in form affect the meaning of each sentence? Respond in ASL.

   This exercise should be fairly easy for most students. You can do it in a group format. This is a good way to emphasize how a change in form can change the meaning.

2. Change the negated sentences into questions. How does this change in form affect the meaning of the sentences? How does the meaning compare with the original sentence that you created? Respond in ASL.

   This exercise builds on the previous one. It is a good exercise to see whether students can manage negation and question forms and still evaluate how these changes in form affect meaning.

Progress Tracking Sheet

Use this sheet to track your progress with the exercises you have completed. After performing the exercise (one or two times) and answering the study questions, fill in the tracking sheet. Note the date that you completed the exercise and give an indication of your level of accomplishment. You can use either a quantitative or a qualitative approach to track your progress.

Exercise Number	Date	First Performance	Study Questions	Questions and Reminders	Date	Second Performance
Exercise 6.1 Quantitative						
Qualitative						
Exercise 6.2 Quantitative						
Qualitative						
Exercise 6.3 Quantitative						
Qualitative						
Quantitative Totals						

UNIT
7

Meaning and Visual Form

There are two goals for this unit. One is to highlight the difference between meaning conveyed in ASL and in a graphic visual form (pictures). The second goal of the unit is to develop visualization as a specific tool in the interpretation process. There are four factors in this unit to consider with regard to meaning and form. The factors are the picture, the ASL, the visualization, and the meaning that the forms share. This unit emphasizes the fact that the form of a message can take various shapes while the meaning can remain constant. This unit builds on the understandings you gained in Unit 6 when you explored the relationships between form and meaning. In this unit you will deepen your understanding of these important concepts by working in the opposite direction. Here you will watch an ASL source text and create a visualization.

This unit includes practice watching ASL and creating an image, either on paper or solely in your mind as a visualization. Nancy Schweda Nicholson (1996) calls the "visuospatial sketchpad" the place where images are created in the mind's eye. The visuospatial sketchpad is an important tool for interpreters to develop and use effectively. Often when an image is visualized, it is remembered better. Sometimes visualization can help in setting up spatial relationships between objects or people referred to in the discourse.

As you practice watching the ASL source sentences (form) in the context of the simple stories provided, you will see through class discussions that no two people envision the same things (meaning), even though all participants are watching the same signed message. This is the converse of what you discovered in Unit 6 in which you saw that even though other people in your class or study group looked at the same pictures (meaning), it is very unlikely that any two people would create the same sentence (form). The words or signs you use to express an idea or the visualizations you develop to remember are a reflection of your language proficiency and the context.

In the video for this unit, Anne Marie looked at the same pictures that you will work from in this unit and provided ASL sentences in response to what she saw. Watch her ASL sentences and create your own visualization based on what you see her signing. Then you will compare your visualization with the picture that Anne Marie looked at when creating her sentences.

Group discussions after the exercises will reveal that there are almost as many different visualizations as there are participants. Some of those differences will be based on assumptions and some will be based on what was actually signed. Keep the topics from the previous unit, especially fidelity, in mind as you proceed to the exercise in this unit. The main topics for this unit are listed here.

Visualization

Visual form

ASL form

Meaning

Explicit and implicit information

Visualization

Visualization is the creation of a "scene" or picture in your mind's eye. This is the process that allows you to see an ASL message and visualize where the items or persons are located in relation to each other. Remember that ASL establishes locations for actors and objects in signing space and that correct use of space is important. For example, once an actor or object is referred to in a specific location, it is necessary to be consistent and know that a particular aspect of space is "occupied" until you reassign that actor or object to another location.

Visualization skill has two important sub-components. One is visualizing the relationships between things or people that you already know, but are not visible at that moment. The other subcomponent is imagining relationships between items or people when you have no prior visual knowledge of their spatial relationships. An example of this difference can be seen in imagining yourself interpreting directions from point A to point B when you already know the way and interpreting the same directions when you have never seen either point A or point B or any of the points in between. Visualization is a way to give form to a scene that you know but cannot see or to give form to a scene that you imagine. Once you have established this form in your mind's eye, you refer to it as you proceed through the interpretation. If visualization is done correctly, then the person you have referred to as being on your right remains there throughout the interpretation. Likewise, the other objects or persons that are being spoken about have "assigned places" in your mind and in your interpretation.

Visual Form

Visual form refers to the graphic images that are shown in this unit. The pictures do not have any specific language form attached to them.

ASL Form

The accompanying DVD shows Anne Marie Baer's ASL responses to the nine pictures associated with each exercise.

Meaning

The concept of meaning is an extremely complex one and is not dealt with in depth here. Gonzalez et al. (1991) provide a good description of the role of meaning in the interpretation process. In brief, the concepts that underlie the spoken form or the visual form constitute the meaning. Seleskovitch and Lederer (1989) refer to meaning as the "sense" of a message. Meaning is the idea or concept that one person wishes to convey to another or that is conveyed by a picture or imagined in a visualization.

Explicit and Implicit Information

According to Larson (1984), "Explicit information is information that is overtly stated by lexical items and grammatical forms" (p.38). Implicit information is information that is understood but not necessarily overtly stated. Information may be implicit because of shared prior information or it may be due to the structure of the language.

Interpreters often wonder how much "explaining" is appropriate during the interpretation process. At issue here is information that is clearly understood and available to native signers of the source language that speakers of the target language might not understand. The implicit information could be culturally bound information or it could be information that people share due to a shared history in dealing with a specific subject. If the people involved in the conversation share the same history and understanding of the topic, then the implicit information does not need to be made explicit.

Larson (1984) offers the following explanation of implicit information. "Implicit information is part of the meaning which is to be communicated by the translation because it is part of the meaning intended to be understood by the original writer" (p. 38). When information is implicit due to the nature of the language, it is necessary to make the information explicit in order for the interpretation to be accurate. This is not explaining or expanding the message, this is simply using the appropriate strategies to preserve the meaning of the message.

The Role of Creating Visual Forms in Response to Signed Information

Interpreters work between spoken languages or between signed and spoken languages. Schweda Nicholson (1996) says that the visuospatial sketch pad is a construct that can assist in developing memory and accuracy in interpretation. To develop memory the interpreter must hear or see the incoming message or source language and perform various mental manipulations to free the message from its original form. One way to do this is to create a visual image.

Sometimes you do not know whether the object the signer is referring to is to the right or left of the signer. It is sometimes crucial to know the actual location of objects or persons in relation to each other, and at other times it is sufficient to know simply that things are in relation to each other. If you sense that the exact relationship is important, then you may need to ask the signer for clarification. Examples of instances where this kind of information is essential could include situations where directions are being given to create something, such as a recipe or a building plan. Another instance where it is important to know the actual relationship is legal testimony, where the exact relationship and location of persons and objects can be very important.

The exercises in this unit encourage you to realize that you automatically visualize situations without realizing it and that the visualizations may or may not match the actual event being referred to. Your mind constantly creates hypotheses about what the signer means and about what the signer might sign. While the creation of hypotheses is important, it is also important to realize that not all hypotheses will be borne out. It is a mark of a skilled interpreter to realize that there may be more than one possible hypothesis and that one or more may need to be discarded in order to convey the meaning intended by the signer. By becoming aware of the visualization process you can capitalize on it and use it to help you improve your memory skills, which in turn will support your interpreting skills.

Discussion Questions

Discuss the following questions with your students to promote insight and increase awareness of the role of visualization in the interpretation process.

1.   *How does visualization relate to the interpretation process?*

     Visualization is crucial to the interpretation process and it is important to take time to encourage students to develop this skill. Creating a visual image in response to a signed message can be a powerful tool to aid the interpreter's memory. It is easier for the interpreter to create and remember a visual image than try to remember all the signs they saw. It is important that the interpreter re-member what was signed. The interpreter cannot interpret what he or she can-not remember. Visualizing the relationships between actors and objects can be a great asset for the interpreter. Accurate visualization skills combined with mem-ory skills reduce the effort needed for the process and reduce the errors in the product.

2. *How does the visualization process used in everyday life differ from that used for interpreting?*

   People often do not really attend to what they are seeing and as a result do not often try to visualize accurately. However, people tend to think they have seen and visualized correctly. Encourage students to realize that the kind of visuali-zation and memory skills used in everyday conversations are not the same as the level of intense visualization and memory that must be used in the interpre-tation process. The first step in accurate visualization is intense, effortful at-tending. Visualization is not an innate process. It can be learned and developed with specific effort. By developing this skill, less effort will be needed later dur-ing the more demanding process of simultaneous interpretation.

3. *What happens when the interpreter does not visualize the message correctly, but thinks that he or she has visualized correctly?*

   The product will most likely be skewed and the interpreter will not realize it. It is possible that an inaccurate visualization will not affect the message. In some cases the actual location of the objects or actors referred to will be inconsequen-tial. It may not matter that Mr. Jones was on Mr. Smith's left and the interpreter visualized Mr. Jones on Mr. Smith's right. However, the interpreter cannot know in advance whether the location of the actors and objects in the discourse is cru-cial or not. It is best to bring this kind of possible discrepancy to the attention of your students and encourage them to note that this kind of discrepancy or ambi-guity can lead to a skewed interpretation and that it is best to ask for clarifica-tion, when possible.

4. *What happens when the interpreter does not correctly visualize the signed mes-sage and he or she realizes that they have not correctly visualized the message?*

   Ideally, the interpreter will stop the signer and ask for a repetition. Encourage students to realize that it is common to gain understanding of the relationships between actors and objects and events during the interpretation process. It is possible and likely that an interpreter's understanding of the crucial relation-ships in a discourse can change as he or she becomes more familiar with the events as described by the signer. In case the interpreter has misunderstood based on a faulty visualization, then the interpreter can create a repair, or re-vised interpretation, of the crucial aspects of the relationship. This kind of repair "mid-stream" may require that the interpreter interrupt the signer momentarily to have time to create the repair.

EXERCISES IN ASL VISUALIZATIONS

Decide whether you want to conduct this exercise in class or whether you want the students to do this exercise on their own time. Use the first exercise as a warm-up and the second and third exercises for out-of-class assignments. If students do this exercise on their own, they must have their own copies of the source material. This exercise can be done in a group setting. Students respond by writing or drawing.

If you decide to conduct this exercise during class time, be sure all the students can see the TV monitor you are using. Ask the students to prepare themselves to attend carefully. Remind them not to write or draw while watching. Ask all students to refrain from making noise during the time the video is being played.

Read the directions and explain them to the students. Allow time for questions after you have given the directions. You should plan on at least 5 minutes to prepare the students for the exercise. Five minutes should be enough if you have the group's attention and if all equipment is ready and in working order.

The exercises in this unit are designed to increase awareness of the importance of visualization and the difference between implicit and explicit information. Some of the information conveyed by the pictures may be assumed to be implicit by some signers or may be considered explicit by other signers. In these exercises, the goal is to clarify the difference between meaning and form when the form presented is ASL.

Here are the factors in the exercises.

The picture or visual form.

The ASL form.

The visualization derived from that picture.

The meaning that these three share.

A native user of ASL was instructed to create a response or sentence that conveys the meaning shown in the picture or visual form. The visual form that the signer looked at is shown in each exercise. You will create your own visual form (visualization) after you watch the signer. Later, as you compare your visualizations to the pictures, it will become clear that the meaning of the pictures can and will be expressed in slightly different forms, depending on the way a person chooses to sign.

Even though you and the signer are looking at the same pictures, it is unlikely that any two sentences or any two visualizations for a specific picture will be exactly the same. Thus, the form is different, and the meaning remains constant. It is true that variations in expression can slightly alter the meaning. The amount of difference in meaning is one of the judgments you will be asked to make as you work through the exercises. Through practice you can become adept at making decisions about whether you have preserved the message. These short scenarios do not contain contextual or cultural information. Additional context can be devised in order to provide more variety in these exercises.

The signer chosen for these exercises has much in common with the speakers used for *The Effective Interpreting Series: English Skills Development*, such as gender, approximate age range, and educational level. The signer did not rehearse her responses in advance of the taping. This allowed for a more spontaneous rendition of the meaning. Please note that the signer's version is not considered "right," rather, each sentence represents the signers' view and manner of expression.

As you practice your visualization skills based only on what is signed, you will notice that sometimes the details that you create in your mind's eye vary depending on your visualization skills. Sometimes details are added that can't be determined from the pictures. This kind of addition is usually based on assumptions. It is important to create a visualization that is as accurate as possible so as not to skew or distort the message. Another common error is to leave out information that was stated. These kinds of additions and omissions are common. Sometimes they are minor and do not create a significant difference in the meaning. You will need to decide whether any of these omissions or additions substantially change the meaning of the messages that you will be working with in this unit.

In summary, here is the process to keep in mind as you work through the exercises. Anne Marie looked at the nine pictures for each exercise. She signed a single sentence for each picture. You will be watching her signing and creating a visualization based on your understanding of her signing. You will represent your visualization with a drawing. Then you compare your visualization (represented by your drawing) with the original picture. Through this process you will sharpen your understanding of two key points.

1. Each person will create a different visualization depending on background knowledge and comprehension skills.

2. Each manipulation of the message (from picture to sign, from sign to visualization, from visualization to drawing) will affect the meaning. Additions and omissions will affect the meaning. This simple exercise helps you to understand the importance of remaining as faithful as possible to the original message.

EXERCISE 7.1

Doing the Laundry

ANNE MARIE BAER

If you notice students are struggling to understand this information sentence-by-sentence, have them watch all nine sentences before creating their visualization and sketch.

Directions

Student Workbook
page 126

Find this video selection on your DVD. Do not look at the printed pictures yet. Watch Anne Marie describe each of the nine pictures in the sequence. After each sentence, pause the DVD. Visualize the images she is describing. Create a mental visualization and draw a quick sketch that represents what she signed. Keep track of the spatial relationships she establishes between actors and objects. Do not worry about your artistic ability; simply make a quick line drawing. Stick figures are fine. Do not write or say any English words to help you remember what she signed.

Study Questions

1. Watch each of Anne Marie's nine sentences. In the space provided below make a quick sketch that represents the visualization you have envisioned based on what Anne Marie signed.

1.	2.	3.
4.	5.	6.
7.	8.	9.

You should expect that no two people have the same visualization. You can ask students what influenced their memory of what they saw. Did comprehension difficulties affect the visualizations that were created? Help your students understand that although there are wide variations in visualizations, many can be acceptable. The important thing is that students can realize that their visualization may or may not be accurate but can be used as a starting point for hypothesis testing.

2. Look at each of the pictures on page 153. Compare your visualizations (represented by your drawings) with the actual pictures. Differences might be due to information that is either missing or added by the signer, to information that you assumed was included but was not, or to information you did not fully comprehend. For each of the nine pictures decide whether your visualization is the same or different from the actual picture. Write "same" or "different" in the numbered spaces below.

In working with students on this question and the one that follows, avoid discussions of drawing ability or lack of drawing ability. If the student responds quickly and moves to these study questions directly, he or she should be able to remember what image they were able to create, in his or her mind's eye, whether he or she was able to draw it or not. Next, the student should make a comparison between the visual image in his or her mind's eye and the visual image presented in the book. The visual image created on paper should be a prompt or cue to help remember what was visualized. It is important to avoid using written English as a visual prompt. The idea is to see what kind of access the student has to creating a non-linguistic or pictorial image in his or her mind's eye in response to an ASL message. To promote discussion about the differences the students found between their visualizations and the actual picture, ask them to provide short descriptions of the differences they noted. These descriptions can be recorded or can be part of an in-class discussion.

	Same	*Different*
Sentence 1		
Sentence 2		
Sentence 3		
Sentence 4		
Sentence 5		
Sentence 6		
Sentence 7		
Sentence 8		
Sentence 9		

3. Refer to your answers to Question 2. For each one of these differences, refer to the video selection and review it to determine which part of her utterance led you to create a visualization that differed in meaning from the original picture. Note your answer in the space provided.

_____

_____

_____

4. Study Anne Marie's responses and then look at each picture and record a sentence for each. Record your sentences, following features you observe in her work to achieve greater fluency and to improve your ASL syntax.

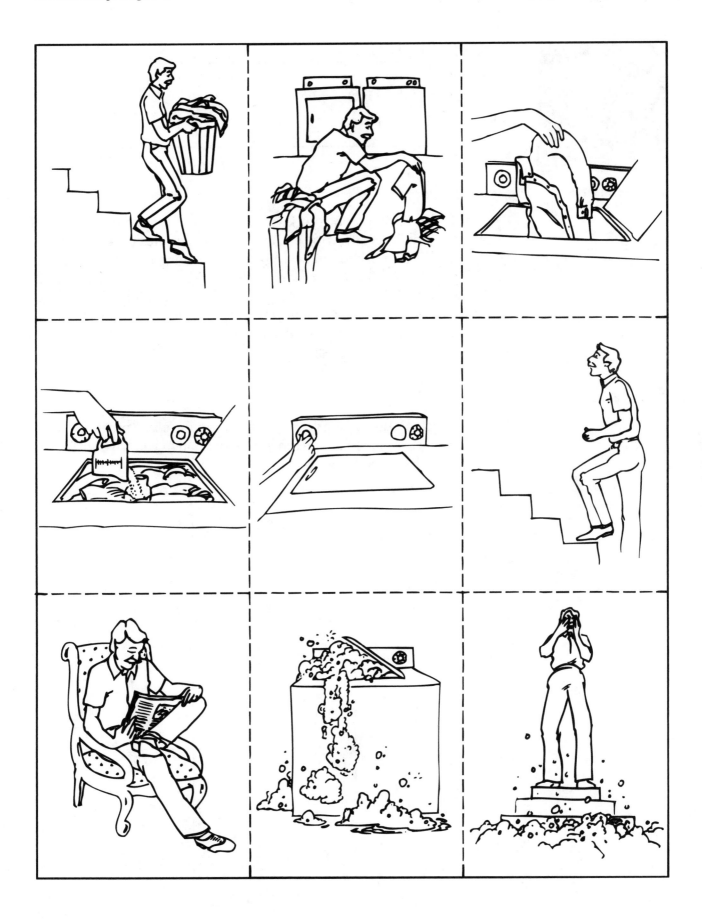

EXERCISE 7.2

Making a Cake
ANNE MARIE BAER

Directions

Student Workbook
page 130

Find this video selection on your DVD. Do not look at the printed pictures yet. Watch Anne Marie describe each of the nine pictures in the sequence. Pause the DVD after each sentence. Visualize the images she is describing. Create a mental visualization and draw a quick sketch that represents what she signed. Keep track of the spatial relationships she establishes between actors and objects. Do not worry about your artistic ability; simply make a quick line drawing. Stick figures are fine. Do not write or say any English words to help you remember what she signed.

Study Questions

1. Watch each of Anne Marie's nine sentences. In the space provided below make a quick sketch that represents the visualization you have envisioned based on what Anne Marie signed.

1.	2.	3.
4.	5.	6.
7.	8.	9.

2. Look at each of the pictures on page 156. Compare your visualizations (represented by your drawings) with the actual pictures. Differences might be due to information that is either missing or added by the signer, to information that you assumed was included but was not, or to information you did not fully comprehend. For each of the nine pictures decide whether your visualization is the same or different from the actual picture. Write "same" or "different" in the numbered spaces below.

	Same	*Different*
Sentence 1		
Sentence 2		
Sentence 3		
Sentence 4		
Sentence 5		
Sentence 6		
Sentence 7		
Sentence 8		
Sentence 9		

3. Refer to your answers to Question 2. For each one of these differences, refer to the video selection and review it to determine which part of her utterance led you to create a visualization that differed in meaning from the original picture. Note your answer in the space provided.

_____

_____

_____

4. Study Anne Marie's responses and then look at each picture and record a sentence for each. Record your sentences, following features you observe in her work to achieve greater fluency and to improve your ASL syntax.

EXERCISE 7.3

The Wading Pool

ANNE MARIE BAER

Directions

Student Workbook
page 133

Find this video selection on your DVD. Do not look at the printed pictures yet. Watch Anne Marie describe each of the nine pictures in the sequence. Visualize the images she is describing. Pause the DVD after each sentence. Create a mental visualization and draw a quick sketch that represents what she signed. Keep track of the spatial relationships she establishes between actors and objects. Do not worry about your artistic ability; simply make a quick line drawing. Stick figures are fine. Do not write or say any English words to help you remember what she signed.

Study Questions

1. Watch each of Anne Marie's nine sentences. In the space provided below make a quick sketch that represents the visualization you have envisioned based on what Anne Marie signed.

1.	2.	3.
4.	5.	6.
7.	8.	9.

2. Look at each of the pictures on page 159. Compare your visualizations (represented by your drawings) with the actual pictures. Differences might be due to information that is either missing or added by the signer, to information that you assumed was included but was not, or to information you did not fully comprehend. For each of the nine pictures decide if your visualization is the same or different from the actual picture. Write "same" or "different" in the numbered spaces below.

	Same	*Different*
Sentence 1		
Sentence 2		
Sentence 3		
Sentence 4		
Sentence 5		
Sentence 6		
Sentence 7		
Sentence 8		
Sentence 9		

3. Refer to your answers to Question 2. For each one of these differences, refer to the video selection and review it to determine which part of her utterance led you to create a visualization that differed in meaning from the original picture. Note your answer in the space provided.

_____

_____

_____

4. Study Anne Marie's responses and then look at each picture and record a sentence for each. Record your sentences, following features you observe in her work to achieve greater fluency and to improve your ASL syntax.

Progress Tracking Sheet

Use this sheet to track your progress with the exercises you have completed. After performing the exercise (one or two times) and answering the study questions, fill in the tracking sheet. Note the date that you completed the exercise and give an indication of your level of accomplishment. You can use either a quantitative or a qualitative approach to track your progress.

Exercise Number	Date	First Performance	Study Questions	Questions and Reminders	Date	Second Performance
Exercise 7.1 Quantitative						
Qualitative						
Exercise 7.2 Quantitative						
Qualitative						
Exercise 7.3 Quantitative						
Qualitative						
Quantitative Totals						

References

Arjona, E. (1984). Education of translators and interpreters. In M. McIntire (Ed.), *New Dialogues in interpreter education. Proceedings of the Fourth National Conference of Interpreter Trainers Convention* (p. 1–36). Silver Spring, MD: Registry of Interpreters for the Deaf.

Baker, M. (1992). *In other words: A coursebook on translation.* New York: Routledge.

Baumann, J. (Ed.) (1986). *Teaching main idea comprehension.* Newark: International Reading Association.

Beekman, J, & Callow, J. (1974). *Translating the word of God.* Grand Rapids, MI:Zondervan.

Bell, R. (1991). *Translation and translating.* New York: Longman.

Bradley (1981). Overconfidence in ignorant experts. *Bulletin of the Psychonomic Society,* 17, 82–84.

Conference of Interpreter Trainers (1998). CIT position paper: Instructional class size- interpreter training, 18 (3), 21.

Cunningham, J., & Moore, D. (1986). The confused world of main idea comprehension. In J. Baumann (Ed.). *Teaching main idea comprehension.* Newark: International Reading Association.

Danks, J., et al. (Eds.) (1997). Cognitive processes in translation and interpreting. *Applied Psychology,* Vol. 3. Thousand Oaks, CA: Sage Publications.

Daro, V., & Fabbro, F. (1994). Verbal memory during simultaneous interpretation: Effects of phonological interference. *Applied Linguistics,* 15, 365–381.

DeGroot, A. (1997). The cognitive study of translation and Interpretation. In J. Danks et al. (Eds.), *Cognitive processes in translation and interpreting.* Thousand Oaks: Sage Publications.

Ericsson, K. (2001). Expertise in interpreting. *Interpreting: International Journal of Research and Practice in Interpreting, 5* (2), 187–221. Amsterdam: John Benjamins.

Ericsson, K. (1996). The acquisition of expert performance: An introduction to some of the issues. In K. A. Ericsson (Ed.), *The road to excellence: The acquisition of expert performance in the arts and sciences, sports, and games.* (pp. 1–50). Mahwah, NJ: Earlbaum.

Ericsson, K. et al. (1993). The role of deliberate practice in the acquisition of expert performance. *Psychological Review, 100,* 363–406.

Gerver, D. (1976). Empirical studies of simultaneous interpretation: A review and a model. In R. W. Brisling (Ed.), *Translation: Applications and research* (pp. 165–207). New York: Gardner Press.

Gile, D. (1995). *Basic concepts and models for interpreter and translator training.* Philadelphia: John Benjamins.

Gonzalez, R. et al. (1991). *Fundamentals of court interpretation: Theory, policy and practice.* Durham, NC: Carolina Academic Press.

Hoffman, R. (1997). The cognitive psychology of expertise and the domain of interpreting. *Interpreting, 2* (1/2), 189–230.

Kearsley, G. (1976). Questions and question asking in verbal discourse: A cross-disciplinary review. *Journal of Psycholinguistic Research, 5* (4), 355–375.

Keiser, W. (1978). Selection and training of conference interpreters. In D. Gerver & H. Sinaiko (Eds.), *Language, interpretation and communication* (pp. 251–257). Amsterdam: John Benjamins.

Kintsch, W. (1972). Notes on the structure of semantic memory. In E. Tulvig & W. Donaldson (Eds.), *Organization of memory.* New York: Academic Press.

Kitano, H. (1993). La traduction de la langue parlee. In A. Clas & P. Bouillon (Eds.), *La traductiuque: Edues et recherches de traduction par ordinateur* (pp. 408–42). Montreal: Les Presses de l'Universite de Montreal.

Klemp, G., & McClelland, D. (1986). What characterizes intelligent functioning among senior managers? In R. J. Sternberg & R. K. Wagner (Eds.), *Practical intelligence: Nature and origins of competence in the everyday world.* (pp. 31–50). Cambridge, MA: Cambridge University Press.

Kohn, K, & Kalina, S. (1996). The strategic dimension of interpreting. *Meta, 41* (1), 118–138.

Krampe, R., & Ericsson, K. (1996). Maintaining excellence: Deliberate practice and elite performance in young and older pianists. *Journal of Experimental Psychology: General, 125,* 331–359.

Larson, M. (1984). *Meaning based translation: A guide to cross language equivalence.* Lanham, MD: University Press of America.

Kitano (1993)

Malakoff & Hakuta (1991). In J. Danks et al. (Eds.), *Cognitive processes in translation and interpreting.* Thousand Oaks, CA: Sage Publications.

Massaro, D., & Shlesinger, M. (1997). Information processing and a computational approach to the study of simultaneous interpreting. *Interpreting: International Journal of Research and Practice in Interpreting, 2,* 13–53.

Moser-Mercer, B. (1978). Simultaneous interpretation: A Theoretical Model and its Practical Application. In D. Gerver & W. H. Sinaiko (Eds.), *Language, Interpretation and Communication* (pp. 353–368). New York, Plenum Press.

Moser-Mercer, B. (1984). Defining aptitude for simultaneous interpretation. In M. McIntire (Ed.), *New dialogues in interpreter education. Proceedings of the Fourth National Conference of Interpreter Trainers Convention* (p.43–71). Silver Spring, MD: Registry of Interpreters for the Deaf.

Moser-Mercer, (1997) Skill components in simultaneous interpreting. In *http://www.benjamins.com/cgi-bin/t_bookview.cgi?bookid=BTL%2023 Conference Interpreting: Current Trends in Research,* Y. Gambier, D. Gile, & C. Taylor (Eds.), 133 ff.

Patrie, C. (1989). *Fingerspelled word recognition and rapid serial visual processing in hearing adults: A study of novice and expert sign language interpreters.* Ann Arbor, MI: UMI.

Patrie, C. (1994). The readiness to work gap. In E. Winston (Ed.), *Mapping our course: A collaborative venture. Proceedings of the Tenth National Convention Conference of Interpreter Trainers,* Charlotte, NC. (p. 53–56).

Patrie, C. (1997). *Fingerspelled Names and Introductions, A Template Building Approach.* San Diego, CA: DawnSign Press.

Patrie, C. (2000). *The Effective Interpreting Series: English Skills Development,* San Diego, CA: DawnSignPress.

Patrie, C.J., & Johnson, R. E. (In press). *Fingerspelled word recognition through rapid sequential visual processing.* San Diego, CA: DawnSignPress.

Peterson, R. (2002). Metacognition and recall. In C. Roy (Ed.), *Innovative practices for teaching sign language interpreters.* Washington, DC: Gallaudet University Press.

Roberts, R. (1992). Student competencies: Defining, teaching, and evaluating. In E. A. Winston (Ed.), *Student competencies: Defining, teaching, and evaluating* (pp. 1–18). Conference of Interpreter Trainers.

Schweda Nicholson, N. (1996). Perspectives on the role of memory in interpretation: A critical review of recent literature. In M. O'Keefe (Ed.), *Global vision: Proceedings of the 37th Annual Conference of the American Translators Association.* Alexandria, VA. American Translators Association.

Saussure, F. (1966). W. Baskin (Trans.) C. Bally & A. Sechehaye (Eds. in collaboration with A. Riedlinger), *Course in general linguistics.* New York: McGraw Hill.

Seal, B. (1999). Educational interpreters document efforts to improve. VIEWS, 16 (2), 14.

Seleskovitch, D., & Lederer, M. (1989). *A systematic approach to teaching interpretation.* Silver Spring, MD: Registry of Interpreters for the Deaf.

Shreve, G., & Koby, G. (1997). Introduction: What's in the black box? Cognitive science and translation studies. In J. Danks, et al. (Eds.), *Cognitive processes in translation and interpreting* (pp. xi–xviii). Thousand Oaks, CA: Sage Publications.

Smith, T. (1984). Response to Barbara Moser-Mercer on simultaneous interpreting. In M. McIntire (Ed.), *New dialogues in interpreter education. Proceedings of the Fourth National Conference of Interpreter Trainers Convention* (p.43–71). Silver Spring, MD: Registry of Interpreters for the Deaf.

Snell-Hornby, M. (1995). *Translation studies: An integrated approach.* Philadelphia, PA: John Benjamins.

Taylor, M. (2002). *Interpretation skills: American Sign Language to English.* Edmonton, AB: Interpreting Consolidated.

Tommola, J. (1995). Gist recall as an aptitude test in interpreter training. In P. Krawutschke (Ed.), *Connections: Proceedings of the 36th Annual Conference of the American Translators Association* (p. 471–382). Medford, NJ: Information Today.

Van Dam, I. (1989). Strategies of simultaneous interpretation: A methodology for the training of simultaneous interpreters. In L. Gran & J. Dodds (Eds.), *The theoretical and practical aspects of teaching conference interpretation.* Udine: Campnotto Editore.